SENIOR GOLF

Ken

This may help with some of your more egregious golf problems, but don't even dream it will bring you the trophy.

Bob

SENIOR GOLF

✦

IT TAKES BALLS TO RETIRE

Robert Faber
with: Tom Simon
University of Michigan Golf Coach
(Retired)

iUniverse, Inc.
New York Lincoln Shanghai

SENIOR GOLF
IT TAKES BALLS TO RETIRE

iUniverse books may be ordered through booksellers or by contacting:

iUniverse
2021 Pine Lake Road, Suite 100
Lincoln, NE 68512
www.iuniverse.com
1-800-Authors (1-800-288-4677)

ISBN-13: 978-0-595-35041-4 (pbk)
ISBN-13: 978-0-595-79746-2 (ebk)
ISBN-10: 0-595-35041-0 (pbk)
ISBN-10: 0-595-79746-6 (ebk)

Printed in the United States of America

Contents

INTRODUCTION xi

CHAPTER 1   GOLF AS THERAPY 1

CHAPTER 2   THE APPROACH 9

CHAPTER 3   BACKGROUNDS 13

CHAPTER 4   THE MIND GAME 21

CHAPTER 5   PREPARING FOR ACTION 35

CHAPTER 6   THE BASIC GAME 41

CHAPTER 7   THE SWINGING GAME 55

CHAPTER 8   THE LONG GAME 77

CHAPTER 9   THE SHORT GAME 82

CHAPTER 10   THE PUTTING GAME 102

CHAPTER 11   COURSE MANAGEMENT 114

CHAPTER 12   IN A NUTSHELL 120

CHAPTER 13   REFLECTIONS 127

CHAPTER 14   ORIGINS OF THE GAME 134

CHAPTER 15   PLAYING BY THE RULES 138

CHAPTER 16   VARIATIONS IN THE GAME 150

CHAPTER 17   DEMOGRAPHICS 158

CHAPTER 18   STATISTICAL TABLES 162

CHAPTER 19   THE EQUIPMENT 169

CHAPTER 20   RESOURCES......................... 180

CHAPTER 21   GLOSSARY OF GOLF TERMS 189

THIS BOOK
The Why and The What Of It

This book is about golf, but is equally applicable to wofodworking or music-making or knitting or writing—to whatever constructive activity works to engage the body and excite the imagination. It is a book that hopes to rekindle spirits muted by the void of retirement, to replace the inertia of idle observation with the satisfaction of participation and to give pleasure and purpose to lives grown dim. There are many paths to revitalization and golf is simply one among many...although perhaps a bit more engaging than most.

It is a well accepted maxim that Man cannot live by bread alone...but neither can he simply rely on the memories of happier, more exciting yesterdays. To a large extent, late-in-life pleasures are tied to the anticipation of more stimulating or productive tomorrows. It is the purpose of this book to encourage those who may have quit too soon to rejoin the struggle and seek new challenges.

This book hopes to inspire older, at least reasonably mobile retirees to do more than sit and watch television and mourn days that once were or might have been. It is a book that suggests golf as one of the more fulfilling alternatives to inertia and offers instructions to help make the pursuit of the game both satisfying and successful.

Bob Faber

ACKNOWLEDGMENTS

Struggling through six decades of bad golf, finally to improve to the point that I dare and do write a book about it, then to have that book published—clearly I could not have done it alone. Even aside from my instructor, Tom Simon, the man with all the answers to all the questions about golf, I had to have help. So, in addition to the wonderfully cooperative fates that have thus far spared me some of the downsides of aging, whom do I thank?

Well, to begin, I guess I owe something to the health care industry, or perhaps to my genetic makeup, or maybe simply to the plain dumb luck that has kept me going beyond the biblical "three score and ten"—one or all of which has kept me and my interests alive and made possible my continued pursuit of adequacy in golf and skiing and tennis.

And my monthly Social Security check should come in for some of the credit as well. Golf and skiing, after all, are not welfare sports.

The National Golf Foundation, represented by Judy Thompson and Jim Kass, has been very gracious in allowing me to reprint the statistical tables they had formulated and that are now included in the appendix of this book, so to it and to them I am grateful.

And the artist's pen of Marti Naudi helps give visual substance to Tom Simon's instructions on some of the right and wrong ways to swing a golf club, so to her my gratitude for helping bring it all to life.

I thank the golf-playing members of my Thursday Night Poker Game—by name Ken Warner, Dick Dougherty, Reynold Lowe, Jarvis Franzblau, Paul Sweeney, Peter Steiner (and even Paul Courant, a nongolfer who endures our poker-table conversations about golf with ill-concealed impatience)—who are blessedly uncritical and who have continued to play golf with me over the years despite my competitive short-comings. I thank them for their companionship on the course and for always leaving me carfare at the end of each game—a courtesy not always extended to me at the end of the Thursday night poker sessions.

Particularly notable and dear are those special friends who first joined me on the University of Michigan Golf Course when I came to town in 1954 and who have been part of my foursome and my life for the following five decades—Sid Pollick, Saul Bechek, and again Jarvis Franzblau. Sadly, an irreplaceable void was left in our foursome and in our lives by Saul's death several years ago.

And it is my kids—David, Mike and Suzy—whose continuing patience and blind filial loyalty have allowed me to really believe that I was as good at those various athletic activities as I pretended or fantasized, so to them—and for their love—I am endlessly grateful.

But without question, the hero of this effort has got to be my wife, Eunice, who has borne with an admirable, if not always silent, stoicism my decades of playing and bragging and exaggerating and complaining and—perhaps worst of all—recounting the exploits of each round. It is with pleasure—and with a deep and abiding love—that I can now assure her that it finally *did* all come together, that I really *did* get it

Bob Faber

INTRODUCTION

Getting Into The Swing of Retirement

When I was young I revered Benny Goodman as the King of Swing. Now I'm older and wiser and I have my values straight. Music may help soothe the savage beast, but it's the slice or the shank or the whiff that probably enraged the beast in the first place, so my revised list of candidates for King of Swing includes Tiger Woods and Vijay Singh and Ernie Ells and other such giants in the world of golf.

The basis for my upgraded respect for the smooth swingers and straight and heavy hitters is the prolonged slump in my game. I am now in my late-seventies and have been playing the game of golf for more than fifty years, but it has only been during the past season that I have finally been able to break a hundred.

Those decades of stagnation didn't really bother me too greatly because I was wise enough and cautious enough to keep my day job, but even for one as dilatory as I am there comes a time to move off the dime. It's true that I've been playing at this game for a very long time, but my recent retirement has given me the time and incentive to take it seriously. I finally *had* to take it seriously because of the embarrassment of my 36 handicap and because I could no longer afford the financial luxury of being a bad but optimistic golfer. Before my retirement I was discomfited but not distraught by losing money to all my friends on the course, losses that were exacerbated by an irrational confidence (one good shot and I was convinced that I had turned the corner) that impelled me to double-press (that is, add a new bet twice the size of the original, but for just the remaining holes) going into the last hole. Besides, I always figured I could make it up afterward at the gin table. After fifty years of playing and losing at both golf and gin it finally dawned on me that it wasn't working. Now that I'm retired and no longer have a salary and have discovered that my social security doesn't provide enough of a financial cushion for me to be casual about my losses, I have finally, if belatedly, concluded that I'd better learn the game or leave it.

I have decided to learn it.

After decades of degrading inadequacy, I have finally worked my way up to mediocre, now consistently playing in the mid-nineties with confidence that the eighties are right around the corner.

I am convinced that anybody who can survive childhood and middle age can learn to swing a club, even though it took me the better part of a long lifetime to prove it. Just in time, too. My wife swore she would leave me if once more she heard that "I've got it now, I really think I've got it," an optimism that was probably rooted in the genes. My mother died just weeks before her 90th birthday, still playing eighteen holes of golf three to four times each week. Whenever we spoke she would enthusiastically inform me that "I've finally got my short iron game under control, although my long-distance woods are giving me a little trouble," or "My long game has really come together, but my short-game irons don't seem to be working." It didn't make any difference—nothing ever changed. Meanwhile, she was always convinced that she was on the edge of greatness and was still taking lessons in her late eighties.

The point of this book is to let the average older golfer know what worked for me, what got me out of my fifty-year slump and perhaps to apply it to his or her own game. By absorbing the advice of one of the fine old-time professionals and great teachers, Tom Simon, then restating some of his recommendations in terms that may have significance for aspiring older amateurs, I believe I can provide a genuine service to a whole class of citizens who are desperate for a taste of success—and may perhaps even save a few marriages in the process.

I know, five decades in the making renders my advice a bit suspect, but have a little faith and a lot of patience—good golf really can happen. I can vouch for it. It took more than a while, but once I took playing better golf seriously and got some expert advice, it finally worked for me.

1

GOLF AS THERAPY

Properly nurtured, the aging process can lift wine from palatable to exotic...can transform casual passion into eternal love...can convert a sap-soaked bug into a fossilized treasure. On the other hand, that same time lapse can turn good wine into cheap vinegar and allow unprotected meat to rot.

For aging retirees it all depends on how the newly unrestricted surplus of time is massaged and manipulated and nourished. Growing old, after all, isn't all that hard—you live long enough and anybody can do it. It's retirement, the art and skill of productively managing all those unleashed hours, that can be so difficult to handle.

There are now close to 36 million retirees in the United States. Some use the leisure of retirement to pursue hobbies held in limbo during the long trip to senior status. Others find satisfaction in volunteering in one of their community's many service organizations. Many are thrilled just to catch up on reading long deferred by the time constraints of work (my wife's father used to complain of being 200 years behind in his reading). Unfortunately, too many of us are simply and sadly beginning to fade from disuse.

In his biography, *I'm Not Done Yet*, Edward Koch, former mayor of New York, mourns for his father who retired too soon, quickly becoming a sad and empty shell with those "vacant and teary eyes you sometimes see in older people when there's no longer much of substance going on in their day-to-day lives."

Koch blames this terrifying condition on retirement, complaining that "We live in a society that has a built-in obsolescence. It comes in arbitrarily, at sixty-five. What's tragic is that those older workers...are typically cast aside unprepared. We don't get lessons in how to handle ourselves outside the workplace....our minds are left to atrophy, while the rest of our bodies are quick to follow."

This is an observation that resonates with my own experience of some years ago when I moved to Ann Arbor, Michigan. I tried to rent a store for a new business I intended to open, but there were no vacancies on the main street. I had noticed, however, that one of the stores, an old jewelry shop, was dark and gloomy whenever I passed by, so I approached it one day in hopes that it might soon become available. When I went in, an old man, seated behind the counter near the front, arose and turned on an overhead light, asking if he could help me.

"I noticed," I began, "that you don't seem to be terribly busy."

"Busy? Ha! I haven't had a customer in here in weeks."

"Well, then," my pitch continued, "I need a store for a new business, so perhaps you would consider allowing me to take over your lease."

"Then what would I do?" he asked. "Now, every morning I get up and come downtown to open the store, spend the day, then I close up and go home. I have something to do and someplace to go. Without this I would have nothing."

Mayor Koch is right, of course, in recognizing the continuing need for physical and mental stimulation. My only small disagreement is with his concentration on the workplace as the only source of that stimulation. It is not retirement that is so debilitating, after all, not simply missing a full-or part-time job, but the lack of alternative activities to fill those newly empty days. Many of us had been so consumed by the process of making a living and raising children and preparing for old age that we failed to develop the skills or interests necessary to carry over into our leisure years. Now, with days no longer defined by our jobs, we should search out some sort of replacement hobbies or projects to fill our days and restore our enthusiasm for life. And it matters little whether that choice is quietly contemplative or physically energizing, as long as we approach it with some degree of passion.

If you had learned to ski as a youngster, for example, the new parabolic skis make the sport easier than ever to pursue—and with its pleasure undiminished even for oldsters past their prime. (It doesn't hurt, either, that after age seventy lift tickets on most ski mountains vary from cheap to free.)

Tennis is another traditionally youthful sport that remains compatible with the limitations of an aging body—an athletic activity made a bit more accessible by substituting the wily strategies of the seniors for the aggressive play of the youngsters.

Or you can borrow a page from the book of my friend Ron, who had spent his preceding half-century in medical school—first learning, then practicing and teaching—finally retiring to his books and his collection of classical records. For some, reading good books and listening to good music is enough, but Ron needed a bit more stimulation, so at age seventy and without any previous experience Ron bought a violin, hired an instructor and began his Phase Two of life. Now, a decade later, he practices every evening and plays with an amateur string quartet once each weekend and can't wait for each new day to begin.

Or learn a creative skill like woodworking—building toys for your grandchildren or flower boxes for your porch or furniture for your home. Or try recording the highlights of your past on paper so your grandchildren will know from whom and what they come.

But if you don't like tennis, and you can't ski, and your tin ear and stubby fingers rule out music and woodworking, and reading is difficult because of your macular degeneration...wait—there is GOLF.

Golf is an activity with many faces: a competitive sport, a gentle exercise, a psychological warm bath (or occasional cold shower), an opportunity to socialize with friends or even to enjoy the solitude of playing an unhurried game alone.

And, despite the intrusion of some of the less attractive elements of the game, such as clubs thrown in frustration after shots gone awry, or the threat of short-term memory loss when computing a bad hole's score, golf can be a surprisingly therapeutic activity. Even for the truly inept athlete, just the pursuit of a better swing or lower score, with whatever degree of success, can be a stimulating and gratifying experience. All that is required for continuing progress is a fair amount of free time, a competitive spirit and—like the response to the out-of-town visitor's question of how to get to Carnegie Hall—practice, practice, practice.

More than incidentally, this recommendation of golf as a post-retirement activity is hardly limited to men, but is applicable to senior women as well. Those male chauvinist days that forbade women from playing golf on Wednesdays ("men's day") or on weekend mornings when men justified their monopoly of the course as a good time to discuss their "important business deals" are long gone. It is true that senior men still outnumber senior women on the golf course by a rate of about four-to-one, but the gap in those numbers is rapidly closing and promises to move much closer to equality in the coming years.

Part of that change can be attributed to the demographics. Of the roughly 36 million retirees in the United States, a bit over 20 million—*more than one-half*—are women. Even the future of that numerical imbalance is on the side of older women. In the 65-69 age group, women outnumber men by 118 to 100, a statistical gap that increases down the road to a ratio of 241 women to 100 men.

But I suspect the most significant factor in the increased participation of women in the game of golf is the long overdo change in society's biases. Women, after all, have been deeply involved in the sport since Mary, Queen of Scots dominated the game in the mid-16th Century. Opportunities for participation by women have been severely curtailed by the prejudices of even the most advanced societies, but the requisite skills and interest have always been evident. One of the early breakthroughs in the game for women was the organization of the

"Ladies Golf Union Of Great Britain" in the late 19th century. The first "British Ladies Amateur Championship" was conducted in 1893 (for amateurs because there were no professionals) a contest won in 1894 by Margaret Scott (unrelated to "Mary, Queen Of..."). More nearly within our own time frame was the emergence of two of the world's most skilled and celebrated women golfers, Babe Didrickson Zaharias, who won the world title in 1946, and her successor Louise Suggs, who won that title the following year. Babe Didrickson Zaharias achieved an even more striking breakthrough by competing in three men's tournaments in 1945, an accomplishment not to be repeated for 58 years...not a very bright record for a sport of democracy. A side note on Babe's history with the game: in 1945 she was the first person to win the LPGA (Ladies Professional Golf Association) for a *total purse of $14,500.*! Times—they are achanging.

However late, the industry is now becoming increasingly friendly to women, both in the design of equipment and in the greatly increased number and promotion of local and professional tournaments targeting women. And now, as worthy successors to Didrickson and Suggs, are such remarkable rising stars as Annika Sorenstam and Se Ri Pak and Michelle Wie. The future for the women and the industry seems very bright indeed.

And despite that long gap in participation because of racism and sexism, that is one of the joys of golf, that it is anybody's game—at any age, with any degree of skill, at nearly any level of physical well-being. My friend Walter, for example, is in his early seventies and was crippled by a botched operation about twenty years ago. He is able to get around, but slowly and painfully and with an almost total dependence on the aid of two canes and a powerful determination. In order to play golf he must struggle into position, achieve a precarious balance, and stand perfectly still. He then drops both canes, takes a very restricted backswing, strikes at the ball using the snap of his wrists for distance and control and then concludes with a similarly constrained follow-through. Having completed this painful and constricted routine, a fellow player retrieves his canes, helps him back into the cart, and drives him to his next shot. The limited distance of Walter's drives and fairway shots is offset by the accuracy of his short game; his pain and inconvenience is offset by the satisfaction of the accomplishment; and most amazingly, he manages to play *bogey* golf. (As a new golfer some of the terms used in this book may be unfamiliar, in which case I suggest that you refer to the "The Glossary," Chapter 21, whenever necessary. "Bogey" for example, is one stroke over par per hole.)

Or consider Tom P., one member of the foursome playing just ahead of our group in last year's Washtenaw Country Club Invitational Golf Tournament. Even at a distance I was impressed by the quality of his long game, each shot consistently long and straight and powerful, but his play was distressingly slow. After each fairway shot, for example, he would move ever so slowly and deliberately back to the cart for his ride to the next shot. It was only later, having a beer with him at the 19th hole that I discovered he had lost both legs in Vietnam.

WE HAVE A LOT OF COMPANY

The best available estimate is that there are now about 26.8 million Americans of all ages and backgrounds who play the game of golf. Golf has become the major American pastime, supplanting even the time-honored favorites of horseshoes and baseball and dominating more after-dinner conversations than politics or sex (although we have no firm data on that). Deep in the middle of this legion of golfers are those poor souls who answer to the demeaning sobriquet of "senior citizen"—**7,249,000** golfers over the age of fifty, fully one-fourth of the total number of golfers. And, at the very core of those chosen few there is a still more select group of about **2,760,000** competitors who are over the age of 65. Being one of that group, I am less surprised at this number than are my grandchildren who remain astonished that I can still breathe on my own, let alone swing a club and exert a passion over an ill-conceived press or a shot gone bad. As an effectively ageless activity, golf is increasingly attractive to those many older players who steadfastly refuse to retire quietly to their rocking chairs to wait out the end of their contract.

For most of us the time limitations of our pre-retirement days excluded golf as a practical leisure activity. Its egregious time requirements (four hours for a round plus, of course, the mandatory open-ended time at the nineteenth hole for beer and bragging afterward) forced us to bypass the game altogether or to play too infrequently to develop the skills necessary to meet even our own modest goals. With retirement, however, all of that has changed. That crushing deficit of available free time has been transformed into an unwieldy surplus, often becoming our single most abundant and sadly underutilized asset.

This book attempts to put that asset to good use, to fill in some of the gaps in the development of golfing skills as they apply to seniors. It tries to explain the game's guiding philosophy and to offer instructions especially designed for older players new to the game or for those seniors who have played too infrequently to develop a winning or at least a satisfying game.

None of this, however, should be construed as suggesting that senior golf be limited to retired older people without alternative activities. John D. Rockefeller, the fabled financier and founder of Standard Oil and known for his dour devotion to God and company, had no unscheduled time to spare and seemed genetically disdainful of all frivolous pursuits of pleasure. But then in 1889 at age 59, he took up golf for the very first time—and never again left it. He practiced the game with the single-minded enthusiasm that had previously marked his success in the world of business, playing in both winter and summer, traveling the distance between holes on a bicycle when too old to walk, having assistants push the bicycle when too feeble to peddle. By all accounts, the only times in his hectic and spartan life when he found relaxation and pleasure were on the golf course and later at the nineteenth hole while trading highly embellished tales of brilliantly exe-cuted golf strokes with the other members of his foursome.

The primary purpose of this book is to recognize the physical and social benefits of golf and to give both aid and comfort to the many older—often *much* older—amateurs who have taken up the game later in life and who now pursue the sport with an intensity and a joy nor-mally associated with the passion of youth. This book is not intended to compete with that vast inventory of golf instruction books already available, most of which are designed to make us all Ben Hogans, but is written from the perspective of an aging hacker who has played for decades—played *badly* for decades—and who only late in life has emerged from his lifelong slump to join the ranks of improving golfers, like a reinvigorated phoenix rising from the ashes of golfing defeat. This book is intended to help similarly inept aspirants by explaining some of the basics of the game and providing the rationale for continu-ing to play—and to brag and curse and complain—so that even the currently inadequate senior golf enthusiast can join his fellows at the 19th hole to recount and perhaps reinvent the day's winning putts and lucky bounces and chips that dropped and in the telling of other such tall tales of golfing derring-do. And that, too, is part of the game.

There are many thousands of people who share space with me in this category of aging hackers, an expanding breed that still has the pas-sion to exult, the will to excel, and the drive to make the effort—and that's just fine. I know it's a well-worn cliché, but with golf it really is as much the journey as it is the destination…getting there really *is* half the fun.

2

THE APPROACH

The first step toward bringing quality to your game is finding the right instructor. (Correction: that's the second step. As with any addiction, the first step is finally realizing that you need help. Losing more than you can afford each time you go out on the course is a great impetus for that discovery.)

I regularly played with Charlie, a low-handicap golfer who gave me eight strokes a side. (Translation: Spotted me one stoke per hole on all but one of each of the two nine-hole segments.) Charlie owned three pizza parlors, but I'm convinced that I was his primary source of income. Finally one day, whether from a deep sense of moral obligation or the guilt that comes from impoverishing a friend, he advised me to seek help and suggested a name.

Tom Simon had been the coach of the University of Michigan golf team, but had retired five years earlier and now teaches on his own at some of the local golf courses. He told me that he's never been happier because now he can teach the way he likes and criticize as strongly and volubly as he wants—unconcerned about critical reactions from the University bureaucracy or the bruised feelings of his students.

At our first meeting he asked me what I thought was wrong with my game and what kind of help I needed.

"It's nothing serious. I pretty well know what I'm doing, but there are one or two little things that need straightening out."

"Okay, let me see you hit a ball."

With that invitation I hit three or four balls for his analysis. They weren't badly hit, although they didn't soar quite as straight and high as I had wanted.

After watching me closely, Tom thought a bit, then made his pronouncement: "That is probably the worst friggin' swing I have seen in my whole friggin' life." (Incidentally, "friggin'" is not a word in Tom's vocabulary.) I've since met some of Tom's other students, some of whom were so incensed by his unrestrained frankness that they left after the first lesson. I, on the other hand, although slightly depressed that my swing elicited such an outburst, was reassured by it. It was obvious that he was willing, even anxious to express his critical reactions to my game, that he would hold nothing back in order to stroke my sensitive ego. Good! It was also obvious that I needed all the help I could get.

Tom knows the game thoroughly and can quickly and effectively analyze a player's weaknesses and flaws, but one of his more rare and valuable attributes is his reluctance to advise radical changes to a student's grip or stance or swing. His feeling is that to a large extent everything that goes into a golf swing is a matter of personal style and that within reasonable parameters each of us will develop our own—and that's okay. His job, then, is to identify those parameters and work within them.

I think that's wise. Too many of my friends, middle-aged and older, have been the victims of lessons from young golf professionals whose drive to inflict perfection included a complete redesign of the swing—too often precipitating a slide into depression and an outbreak of nervous tics. Chances are that if we're finally seeking lessons at age fifty or older we are probably pretty well set in our ways and unable to accommodate major changes in our swing or our posture or other ingrained parts of our game. Any attempt to force us to forget our old habits and adopt dramatic changes in how we play are probably doomed to failure anyway, and in the process may even exacerbate our problems and further diminish both our confidence and our pleasure.

When seeking professional advice, try to find an instructor with whom you can work in comfortable harmony (seniors, after all, tend to be less malleable and more opinionated than youngsters, so the information absorption process is helped immeasurably by a good sense of compatibility with your instructor) and one with enough maturity to accept the possibility that you may never reach that plateau of excellence that will satisfy the instructor's professional ego or that will measure up to your own unrealistic fantasies, but one who will instead be satisfied with simply leaving you a better golfer at the end of the instructions than you were when you started. It may well be my age bias, but I'm convinced that if wisdom doesn't come with age, at least experience does, and the two are equally beneficial. (That's an age discrimination to which I plead guilty. I keep finding the age of expertise dropping lower and lower, so that although I can live with the embarrassment of seeking the assistance of my five-year-old granddaughter in programming the VCR, I have an especially uneasy sense of vulnerability with doctors who appear to be no older than my teen-aged grandson.) I suspect a good teaching professional who is well into middle-age is more sensitive to the special problems of an older golfer who, after all those years, *still* hasn't made it. He is probably more willing to accept less in terms of high-quality golf results in exchange for significant improvements—whatever the final scores may be.

But a word of caution. When that great moment finally does come, for the sake of your audience try to curb your enthusiasm. There is nothing more boring, after all, than listening to an ex-duffer verbalize his remarkable triumph in endless and excruciating detail. Meanwhile, keep your dreams to yourself. My wife, who has suffered the verbalization of my travails for the past 53 years, without silence or compassion insists, insists that during all that time nothing has changed—not the scores and not the conversation. So we now have a deal: I don't tell her before the game that today I really feel good about my swing, I really think I've got it, and when I come home afterward she doesn't ask how

I played. It seems to work and it just may be enough to keep us together for a few more decades.

3

BACKGROUNDS

Tom Simon's long career in golf can boast of other credits besides pulling me out of my five-decade slump, although perhaps none more challenging. In his early days, in common with most older professionals, he began as a caddie, in his case at the Inverness Golf Club in Toledo, Ohio. (Incidentally, he bemoans the replacement of caddies by golf carts as a sad end of an era when poor kids could learn to love the game and have the opportunity to play it without cost. The hope now is that such outstanding young players as Tiger Woods and fifteen-year-old Michelle Wie will enthuse the coming generation, and that public courses and clinics will make it possible for this new crop of kids to help develop and effectively pursue an interest in the game, replacing for them the benefits that had been available via the caddie system through all the years of the sport until recently.)

Tom's career as caddie began when he was eleven years old and too small to carry the heavy bags of the well-equipped players, but he was nevertheless out on the course every day of the season, struggling under the weight of any bag he could lift and by using the members' clubs, setting course records for his own "personal best" in those few hours between daybreak and the start of the club's reserved tee-times.

Some of the Inverness Golf Club senior members had a very profound effect on young Tom—helping him, advising him, setting standards and goals for him, and generally providing an inspiration that would serve him well into his adult years. A very special few of that select group, probably because of their growing fame and the gracious manner in which they paid heed to the young Tom, continue to stand out as exemplary role models. One was Herman Lang, at the time the assistant to Byron Nelson but who later went on to become one of the country's great golf instructors. Another was Frank Stranahan, a two-time winner of the British Amateur Open, who later turned pro and won a host of tournaments including the Los Angeles Open and the Miami Fourball and built a solid reputation as one of the luminaries of the game.

During those years, however, one player stood out from all the rest, one of the universally recognized and widely respected giants of the game and one whom Tom still reveres—Byron Nelson.

At the time Nelson, a United States Open and Master's Open Champion, was the pro at Inverness and was ranked among the most acclaimed and accomplished players in the nation. Tom may have been too small to carry Nelson's big leather bag, but he was just the right size to shag balls for him, which he insisted on doing whenever the occasion arose. Tom was forever in his shadow—trailing him, emulating his walk and his swing, and absorbing everything The Great Man had to say. Nelson's advice to members of the club on how to play the game found a home in Tom's memory, and Nelson's expertise and the insights of his teaching connected with young Tom in a way that shaped his own game and his future. Even those technical pointers that emerged during casual conversations with members of the club somehow attached themselves to Tom, to surface later during his own practice and play and then again still later during his teaching career. It was that fruitful and fortuitous combination of observation and imitation that wielded the greatest influence on Tom and did more than anything else to shape his philosophy and knowledge of the game.

Unfortunately, Tom's adulation was untempered by common sense, so when Nelson advised one of the members that in order to help keep the head steady during the swing he should try to visualize it being held firm between a couple of two-by-fours, Tom listened and took it literally. That evening in his garage, he traced his head measurements onto a board, nailed several pieces of two-by-fours to the markings of his head size, then nailed the whole contraption to the studs of the wall. He squeezed his head into the reduced opening and commenced swinging a club for the next half hour. Unfortunately, his measurements were a bit too tight, eventually causing his collapse from the pressure of the vise-like constraint. The good news is that the hospital only kept him overnight—and to this day, he holds his head steady as the sphinx when swinging his golf club.

Tom turned pro in 1950—just in time to be hit by the draft for the Korean War (the day he entered his first pro tournament was the day he received his draft notice). Back-to-back 71s in the second golf tournament of his career helped him make the cut, but before he could make full use of it he was inducted into the army, a career shift that kept him occupied for the next few years. When he was discharged in 1952 he resumed his career, first as assistant golf pro at Bay View Golf Club in Toledo, then as assistant golf pro in several clubs in California, including Candlewood Country Club in Whittier, Los Serranos Country Club in Chino, and Wilshire Country Club in Los Angeles, meanwhile touring whenever possible. It was during one of those tours six months after returning from Korea and just before leaving for California that Tom had perhaps his most notable success. In July, 1953, in a tournament at Bayview Country Club in Toledo, he broke the course record by shooting an eight-under-par 60. It was, however, a record that was fated to fall before he had a chance to enjoy it—the very next day he set a new record on the same course by shooting a ten-under-par **58**!

The hiatus caused by his time in the service, followed by some serious health problems, combined to make him give up the game for about a decade, but when he returned to health and to golf he became the golf pro at the University of Michigan and was soon appointed coach of the University's men's golf team. A short time later, he had coach of the Michigan women's golf team added to his list of responsibilities and succeeded in helping them win their very first golf trophy.

His retirement from the university in 1990, rather than reducing his teaching load, gave him the opportunity to teach a wider range of pupils—and the daunting challenge of dealing with students like me.

My own athletic background, unfortunately, was a bit less distinguished than Tom's. My performance on the football field was marked by dropping the ball and missing my tackle with impressive regularity; my basketball was frustrated by the very low-ceilinged court at the local "Y" in which I simply aimed to miss the ceiling and perhaps to hit the rim; and the closest I got to baseball were amorphous games of stickball in an alley too narrow to accommodate a second base, thereby significantly improving my chances of occasionally reaching third.

While Tom's earliest years were largely defined by the rarefied world of golf, my youth, probably because of my inadequate skills and fragile frame, kept me well on the fringe of all activities related to either team or individual sports. As a teenager I became slightly familiar with the game of golf through my father, but his skills then were little better than mine several decades later, so between his athletic ineptitude, his left handed stance and the very limited leisure time we had together, it is hardly surprising that I failed to benefit from his example or instructions. Thus hindered by the circumstances of life, I played very little golf during my teen years and played that rather badly. Like Tom and most young men of that era and earlier, my life, too, was redirected by military service, after which I returned to civilian life and the raising of children and the all-consuming task of trying to make a living. During those years I continued to play golf intermittently, but the quality of my game, always bad, somehow managed to deteriorate. Finally came the devastating realization that it was not my lack of understanding of the game or my shortage of time to practice and play that held me back—it was simply that I was really not very good.

Late in life, however, despite my very limited athletic abilities, I came to appreciate my one distinct advantage over Tom: Even with diligence, dedication and hard work, he was unlikely to shave very many points off his score, but was pretty well stuck in the 70's. I, on the other hand, with my 36 handicap and my almost complete ignorance of the style and techniques necessary for a good golf swing, had an excellent opportunity for massive improvement readily within my reach.

And, too, I had the benefit of being able to call on Tom to help my game.

Tom Simon, (left) with President Gerald Ford at the University of Michigan's "Pro-Am Michigan Open Golf Tournament" in 1978. (The unidentified man in the middle was the groundskeeper.)

Tom Simon with Ben Hogan, one of only five players to win all four Grand Slam titles. Pictured in 1982 at the Fort Worth Banquet where they served together on the Texas Advisory Committee.

Simon-Chiaverini Win Ottawa Tourney With Record 57 Score

7-14-53

By JIM MacDONALD

PROFESSIONALS Tom Simon and Val Chiaverini fired a phenomenal 14-under-par 57 yesterday at Ottawa Park to win the Rick Prentiss best-ball tournament.

The pair, top playing pros in the Toledo district, outdistanced a field of 114 players in setting an all-time best-ball record. Their round included 14 birdies.

In addition, Simon, 25-year-old assistant at Bay View, set an individual tournament mark at Ottawa with a blazing 30-32—62

which included seven straight birds.

Chiaverini, Valleywood pro, coined a 33-33—66. He helped the team with birds on the first, 16th and 18th holes.

Deadlocked with 65s for second place were six teams. They were Don White - Lou Poulos, Arnie Adams - Cal Wilson, Bob Huddleston - Bud Anteau, Leo Kubisk - Tug Wilson, Harry Kasten-Ed Sova and Don Mikol- Cas Operacz.

Tied for third were Charlie Spross - Ed Chiapetta, Walter Wodja - Russ Ostrander, Ed Smith-Merle Hinkle, Ken Close- J o h n Martin, Buddy Smith-

Charlie Smith and Bert Sproule-Ted Losek. They carded 67s.

An additional five combinations were in fourth position at 68.

Simon, who was playing with a new set of irons, bogeyed the first hole but then canned seven birds in a row. He added four more on the back side but missed a chance for a 60 by taking three putts on the final green from about eight feet away.

Jimmy Cramb, the host pro, said the Simon - Chiaverini round was "one of the most remarkable" he had ever witnessed in his many years of golf.

Best amateur score of the day was turned in by husky Bob Huddleston, current Toledo District Amateur champion, who fashioned a 67. Johnny Phillips was second best with a 68.

Proceeds of the tournament were turned over to Prentiss, assistant pro at Ottawa, to help defray hospital bills accrued by his 4-year-old son, Timmy.

Bay View Course Simple For Simon

That course record set Wednesday by pro Tommy Simon at Bay View Park golf course stood less than 24 hours.

Simon shot a 60 then—eight under par.

Yesterday, playing with Gene Eapp and Bill Ellis, he fired a 30-28—58—ten under par. He had nine birdies and an eagle and one bogey.

Simon is assistant pro at Bay View. 7-53

Newspaper reports of two of Tom Simon's victories in July, 1953. The top article refers to his 14-under-par 57 Best Ball course record. The second article recounts his back-to-back pair of solo course records: a 60–8 under par, followed by a 58–10 under par.

4

THE MIND GAME

Golf is **not** a metaphor for life. And despite some of the terminology used in reaction to shots gone bad, it has nothing to do with divinity—unless in recalling and lamenting the biblical trials of Job. Nor for most mortals is it a reasonable road to fame and fortune. It is simply a game.

Well, not *simply* a game. In some ways it is very much more than just a game. It is a continuing challenge, a series of humbling experiences, and a reaffirmation of the imperfectability of Man. It is usually frustrating, often humiliating, and only occasionally satisfying. Even when playing alone, it is a remarkably competitive game and fully capable of inflicting serious damage on even slightly fragile egos. Very simply, it is a sport that seems designed to frustrate the confidence and conceit of the very best of men and women, offering in return little more than the dubious comfort of sharing the misery with hordes of other similarly afflicted participants. (My golf-addicted barber insists the game is called "golf" because all the other four-letter words were already taken.)

It all begins with your attitude when standing up to the ball on the first tee. The ball is just a ball, after all, an inanimate sphere without moods or sensitivity, so appeals to its better nature will avail nothing. On the other hand, unseemly aggression, like trying to pound the damn thing into submission in an attempt to gain the distance and direction of your heart's desire, is an approach predestined to failure (although the value of a sincere plea while still in flight not to hit that tree and to stay out of that pond can't hurt and should not be summarily ruled out).

This advice, incidentally, is more than simply a glib space filler. Setting a mood by concentrating on the ball is actually a valid and important preparation for what is supposed to follow. It helps to establish a suitable frame of mind to accommodate the rhythm and timing necessary for a smooth and effective swing of the club. Golf, of course, is not the only athletic endeavor in which mastery of the mind plays an important role, but it may well be that attitude and mental participation play a greater part in conquering golf than is true in the other sports. The single most constant theme throughout Tom's lessons is that golf, very much more than other games, is a psychological sport, shaped and properly honed by one's mental approaches to it. For the aspiring amateur, a single-minded determination to pound the ball 300 yards down the middle of the fairway, for example, is almost guaranteed to send the ball flying out of bounds or disappearing into a water hazard or, even more embarrassing, still posed proudly and untouched atop the unbroken tee.

But proper control of the mind can be a much more positive and productive procedure than simply restraining its evil impulses and consequent gaffes. Phil Mickelson, for example, winner of two dozen major PGA championships in the last eight years, credits his victory in the Hartford Open (shooting a 9-under-par 61 on the third round) on his new effort at mental discipline, a strategy he shaped and sharpened while browsing through some notes from his old college psychology courses. He realized that "I had been spending a lot of time on my game, but I haven't spent the time and effort mentally preparing," so he began "visualizing what I want to occur [and] pulling off those shots," a tactic that paid off handsomely at Hartford. In brief, the proper swing—assisted by the right grip and stance and weight shift—are all essential to a good game, but at least as important are the attitudes and thoughts that direct that swing.

Once, after having blown a shot for no apparent reason and searching for an easy fix, I asked Tom about the propriety of rotating my hands slightly to the right or of making certain small changes in the plane or speed of my backswing. His perfectly reasonable response, calming some of the fears that had been eroding my confidence and crippling my swing, was, "There's no such thing as the 'proper' or 'improper' way to swing a golf club. There is simply a way for Bob Faber to swing a golf club. In other words, what's good for one person isn't necessarily good for the next person. Everybody has a different style and different physical capabilities." Of course, that's little comfort for those of us with no style and limited capabilities, but it does eliminate the anguish of trying unsuccessfully to fit into a mold designed by young, strong, and supple pacesetters.

It also helps me accept the pre-hit performance of my friend, Miles. Miles has the most convoluted, grotesque preparation for a golf swing that can be imagined. His right leg stretches outward while his hands manipulate a variety of shifting positions on the shaft of the club with the spastic motions of a man totally devoid of muscle control. With his body hunched over and all its individual parts moving in their own contorted and independent ways, all the facets of that bizarre demonstration somehow coalesce into a smoothly executed swing against a powerfully struck ball that finds its way down the middle of the fairway and onto a consistently high-80s scorecard—leaving all his condescending critics in an embarrassed state of bewilderment and dismay. Despite the bizarre maneuvering of all the separate parts of his body and the breaking of all the rules of both golf and logic, he took a hint from the familiar Frank Sinatra song and does it his way—which seems to serve him very well indeed.

Nevertheless, however much room exists for individuality and innovation, a certain few absolutes of the game must be understood and practiced by anyone who intends to take the game at least somewhat seriously and who would escape the devastating embarrassment of a 36-handicap; there are still the basics of the game that must be mastered and incorporated into the swing pattern of each individual golfer, however unique and distinctive the ultimate style.

Volumes of sound advice on those basics, incidentally, can be found in any one of that vast collection of golf instruction books already available in book stores and libraries, but that advice tends toward a concentration on the purity of the ideal swing rather than dealing with the variations necessary to meet the requirements of age-related restrictions. The audience for the majority of those golf books, after all, tend to be either aspiring professional wannabes, or talented amateurs dedicated to reducing an already enviable handicap, or rank beginners whose minds and bodies are still young and strong—none of which represents the special problems of we aging hopefuls.

Nick Faldo, winner of two Masters and three British Opens, for example, recommends in his book *A Swing For Life,* that "at the finish of the swing, wrap the club around your neck." That's good advice, but it does not necessarily apply to older men who strain when tying their shoelaces. The physical limitations of amateur golfers more nearly my age require a much greater attention to all the many individual subtleties of the swing than suggested by the full and powerful action recommended here by Faldo. It is true that all the many small elements of the golf swing play equally crucial roles in everybody's performance, but younger players, not yet degraded by the restrictions of age, may indulge themselves more completely in the fullness and the power of their action without redirecting their concentration away from the various requisites of a good swing. Most older amateur golfers, on the other hand, have to focus more attentively on all those crucial details, blending the rhythm and the timing and the countless other factors into one coordinated whole in order to achieve an acceptable shot.

And that is the philosophy that directs Tom's teaching of the basics. He insists that golf is primarily a mental game, from the concentration on the many small details of the swing, to the psychological preparation for play, to the attitude that colors every move and accompanies the player on every round—and I see no reason to quarrel with that assessment. The remarkable quality of Tiger Woods' game, for example, is rooted in a combination of many factors including his natural skills and his agility and his love of the game, but at least a part of it comes from one particular aspect of his father's training. Whenever young Tiger and his father played together his father would make a point of distracting his son on every shot, talking in the middle of a swing, walking in front of him while he was preparing to putt, altogether being a pain in the stroke during the entire round. The senior Woods is not an inconsiderate parent, but a clever instructor who taught his son the discipline of total concentration.

Tiger's firmly focused mind is as well prepared as his grip and stance and swing. The fact that he recognizes the significance of a well-disciplined mind in the successful pursuit of this sport is evidenced by his comments after losing the British Open to Justin Leonard, referring admiringly to the winner as being "a great player—very, very tough mind," an attitude echoed more recently by Annika Sorenstam, the number one player in the LPGA (Ladies Professional Golf Association) when asked to identify the strongest part of her game: "My mind," which was the same point made, albeit in a different field of athletics, by that sports philosopher Yogi Berra, the famed Yanakee baseball star, who once observed that "90% of the game is mental—the other half is physical."

For older players who are still struggling to gain some degree of mastery over this elusive game, the mental approach is especially important. At one time or another, for example, all of us have probably played with friends who might occasionally dub a drive or skull a mid-iron shot or miss an easy lob to the green and whose reaction is to throw the club or stomp on the ball or at the very least curse and scream and pout—never a pretty sight. The justification for such primitive or juvenile behavior is that it lets off steam, thereby relaxing us and enabling us to resume our natural equanimity in time for our next shot. Great theory, but it just ain't so. The intrusion of that one momentary lapse of concentration, that single instance of a badly botched swing can be enough to seriously disrupt the pattern of our game for the next several holes if we don't act to get it under control immediately. In our effort to compensate for those several lost yards or added strokes, we tend to swing too hard in our determination to gain more distance, or too fast in order to hurry up and test our theory about why that shot went bad, or too wildly because we are convinced our problem was *X,* in which case we become so focused on correcting *X* that we forget about all the other equally important factors that comprise a good swing. There are so many details to be remembered in trying to develop and execute a smooth, well-coordinated golf swing that our concentration will inevitably wander at times. Add to that the confusion of minds further cluttered by the frustrations of shots gone awry and we are in very big trouble indeed, so we must steel ourselves against falling prey to the anger and the tensions of excess anxiety. When you hit a bad shot, whatever else, ***keep your cool.*** Struck the dirt instead of your ball? Hey, it happens. Now forget it.

It's at this point that Tom likes to quote a bit of counseling he once received from Don Canham, the former athletic director at the University of Michigan. In advising Tom about handling a personal problem, Don said, "Don't ever let your emotions overrule your mind." Tom reapplies that advice to golf, insisting that its application is valid and essential. "Don't concentrate on what you did wrong," he says. "You've done it right before, so you know you can do it. Now, just think in terms of repeating what worked in the past." Nothing mysterious, just calm down, compose yourself and let it be fun. Putting the game in its proper perspective should smooth out the rough spots and coheres with his helpful platitude, "Never strike a blow in anger."

A SEARCH FOR CALM

Losing your cool can also be terribly time-consuming. Playing once with Dick, my frequent golf companion, I was struck by the amount of time that had passed since I had last seen him enter the rough in search of his sliced drive. Impatiently awaiting his emergence from the trees bordering the thirteenth fairway, I finally sought him out and found him circling a thicket of trees and looking skyward with an unlikely story to tell. Seems he had a bad shot followed by another bad shot, after which in his frustration he simply "flipped" his club lightly over his shoulder in a mild expression of dismay. A very unlikely story. We spent the next fifteen minutes looking into the trees, searching for the silvery shaft of his 7-iron until the foursome behind us encouraged our move onward. Coming back down the eighteenth fairway (which borders the thirteenth) we stopped to search again, and still again we searched without success. For the next month, every time we played that course we followed the same routine with the same lack of success. It was not until the onset of Autumn and the disappearance of the leaves that the iron finally revealed itself, stuck in the uppermost reaches of a very tall maple tree. It took a dangerous and terrifying climb most of the way to the top, aided by the jostle from a fully extended water-ball retriever, to finally achieve its release. He had just lightly *flipped* it? Not likely. From the evidence of its month-long resting place, it is more likely that he used both hands in a concentrated shot-put heave to accomplish his feat. I doubt that his release of frustrated energy helped restore the equilibrium of his game—I *know* it did nothing for mine.

The sister to keeping your cool is *slow it down—take it easy!* One of the most important aspects of the game, right up there with the grip and the swing, is **patience**. Don't rush to the tee, for instance, but walk to it slowly, then perhaps (certainly on the first tee) establish some sort of stretching routine, a role intended more for the mind than the muscles. Never initiate the swinging action before you have thought clearly and precisely about what you intend to do and how best to accomplish your goals. Before beginning my backswing I have finally learned to simply stand motionless for about five seconds while addressing the ball, thereby establishing a moment of relaxation that enables me to empty my mind of all extraneous matters, reduce some of the mental and muscular tension that had been building, perhaps ease the tight grip with which my left hand had been choking the club—and *then* I begin. A word of caution, however: an excessive delay devoted to reexamining the mechanics of the shot or to pondering the likelihood of error is likely to increase the tension, which in turn is perhaps the single most damaging enemy of a good golf swing.

When I was very young, I was regularly admonished by my mother to "act your age." In middle age the reproof resurfaced when my wife would become distraught over my refusal to recognize the physical limitations of my age (or perhaps the immaturity of my behavior, but that's a different issue altogether). Now I'm getting it again, but this time from Tom Simon. In tennis, the court next to mine is often used by some young squirts slamming the ball with all their considerable strength, disturbing my game with the relentless *thwonk, thwonk, thwonk* as the ball is pounded with all the power those young bodies can bring to bear. It's not jealousy that destroys my game, but emulation. I instinctively identify with their loose, but controlled and supple strength, so, of course, my next shot tangles with the net or flies off the court over the back fence. Unfortunately, the same is true with golf. Watching a golf tournament on television, I marvel at the relaxed rhythm and grace that propels each shot and am convinced that by simply imitating the style of the pros I'll find my key to success. But I cannot, and that is why I'm constantly reminded to act my age. The clubs of those young professionals wrap around their necks on both the backswing and the follow-through, and their power bubbles through their whole body from their toes through their fingers until it is finally released right at the moment of contact with the ball. I didn't have that controlled power when I was their age five decades ago—why in the world should I assume it now?

It is about then, watching the pros on the small screen and struck by the obvious ease and simplicity of the mechanics of a good swing and of the consistent power and controlled direction of the result, that I run out to the course, grandly refuse my competitor's offer of five-strokes-a-side-Nassau (one of a myriad assortment of bets that tends to make the game more costly) and begin—again—the decline into reality: I still don't have it! All those lessons that were just beginning to take hold, all that advice I had absorbed and all that practice on the range—gone. I had become so confident that the newly discovered correction in my swing was the answer to the deeper mysteries of the game that I concentrated on just that single motion to the exclusion of everything else I had learned—and the result was disastrous. Tom,upon hearing my lament and dismissing my self-pitying posture, insists, "You're gonna play and score a whole lot better when you play only up to your capabilities. Don't push it beyond what you can do reasonably well. After all," he says, "it's not the capacity to make *great* shots that makes champions, but the ability to make fewer *bad* shots."

Trying hard and occasionally succeeding is one of the great joys of the game, but trying too hard is much more common and is too often the path to self-inflicted disaster. When Tom advises us to play within the limits of our capabilities he's asking us to stick to what we know we can do and do well, so that we can swing without the anxiety and apprehension that might disrupt our rhythm. Our inclination is to flex our muscles and swing with all we've got in order to pound the ball farther than before—a tactic doomed to failure. Rather than shoot for the moon and miss the fairway, it is better to aim for lesser but more attainable goals and reach them. Playing the game with more modest aspirations until we gain a greater degree of confidence and control enables us to hit the ball with the authority necessary to strike the ball both hard *and* well.

It is true, of course, that confidence can be a rather elusive state of mind for one whose history of shanks and whiffs and mishits can be traced back into the distant decades, but it remains a goal worth pursuing. I'm convinced that one of the reasons young golfers are so much better than older ones—aside from the obvious factors of strength and agility—is their level of confidence. This is particularly true in the short game where delicacy and control are so important. The pessimism that tends to be more natural with age and experience, the awareness that things can and often do go wrong, is one of the many characteristics that distinguish us from our children. In much the same way that older people are aware of mortality (unlike the young who will live forever), the golf shots that uncertain older amateurs approach with trepidation are attacked with fearless abandon by the young. Whereas the confident swing of youth provides a smooth and fluid motion, the fearful concerns of the older players ("I sure hope this little lob clears that trap"...or "I miss this short putt and it's another double-bogey"...or "I skull this chip, it'll fly over the green, then I'm in *big* trouble") tightens our grip and our swing and can be self-fulfilling prophesies.

An example of the impact of confidence gained and lost was my own experience with a new lob wedge, a delicate instrument that I had never used before. It felt so good and performed well so consistently that I assumed I could do no wrong with it, an attitude that encouraged an easy fluid swing that left the ball on the green each time I used it. One day I tried using it for chipping...and sent it bouncing off to the right. I tried it again and missed it again—and still again a number of times afterward. After that, having lost my confidence I was unable to use the club again for lobbing or chipping or any purpose whatsoever for a very long while. Eventually, after a lot more time on the range and another lesson from Tom I was finally able to rekindle some of the confidence that had guided my earlier efforts with that club and, subsequently, some of the old familiar magic of its performance

Tom's confidence-restorative (sounds like something that should be bottled and sold at state fairs like snake oil) extends well beyond advice to me. One of Tom's ex-students, an outstanding young player named Katie, recently called him at midnight from Atlanta. She was in a major tournament, going into the final round, running third behind two members of her foursome—and she was nervous. Something was wrong, but she had no idea what it was or how to correct it. What can she do?

After admonishing her about her more egregious error of calling him at midnight, he followed up with some reasonable and practical counseling: "There are no magic pills or mystical potions for your problem; you've simply got to drive through this thing by yourself. Now, do you think you have it in you to beat these women?" Reassured that she thought she was better than they, he said, "Then just play your game. Get up on the tee, look at them, and think to yourself, 'Here I am—now you beat me.' Make them come to you. Make yourself the one to beat."

It worked. She went on to win the tournament, then came north to win the Michigan Open, scoring a 69 on the first round. The point of all this is to illustrate the importance—at *all* levels of the game—of confidence and a well-controlled mindset. (Freud may have targeted a different group of patients when he refined the practice of psychiatry, but clearly the effective manipulation of the mind can do a lot for golfers.)

So why in the world do we inadequate older golfers continue to seek the punishment of subjecting ourselves to the frustrations and disappointments of the game? Considering the high cost of greens fees and the soaring price of golf clubs and the tendency to upgrade whenever an expensive new piece of equipment comes on the market, players past middle-age must be either logic-deprived or incurably optimistic to continue their efforts. It is the optimism, of course, that finally sustains us. Our several score of poor shots on an average round are easily eclipsed by the memory of that small handful of well-hit balls that stick in our mind. It is those few star-touched shots that are the subjects of our nineteenth hole conversations and that bring us back to the course again and again. To some degree, too, it is our very inadequacy that brings us back for more. When you're shooting scores of 110 or more, it is not that difficult to knock off five strokes or better, so although a score of 105 is not very impressive, for the player who had hit 110 the day before, that degree of improvement is a positive cause for rejoicing. It may not make a lot of sense, but it's a reality of the game—and for those of us who fall into that category it can be very reassuring.

Those 200-yard-plus drives are another victim of the aging process, so by our late fifties most of us should replace the idea of "power" golf with "mental" golf. One of the goals of practicing endless hours on the driving range is to develop "muscle memory" so that the repetition of a few basic motions will in time make that swing automatic, thereby eliminating much of the need to think when swinging at the ball. The trouble is that with increasing age I find that the memory of my muscle is little better than the memory of my mind, which is sometimes very limited indeed. I may remember to bring the club all the way back in a straight line low to the ground, but then I forget to pivot sufficiently or to stretch my left shoulder under my chin. Or I'll remember to pause at the top of my backswing, but forget to follow up with a slowed down-swing. During the past few years, I have tried to mark those moves that are most essential to my swing and that I tend to forget most frequently, then to put them in some sort of form to jog my memory. There are a wide variety of jogs, such as a little jingle:

If you really want to win

Tuck your shoulder 'neath your chin.

After that the thing to do

Is concentrate on follow-through.

or, perhaps an acronym based on techniques to be remembered. such as:
:

M ove slowly

E lbow tucked

S hift weight

S low downswing

or perhaps a dual purpose reminder, such as remembering to move the club **S**lowly on both the takeaway and the downswing, then to **EX**plode through the ball at that moment of contact, a series of movements easily recalled by the identifying letters of the two key instructions...S-EX. That can be an excellent and easily remembered mental jog, but be careful that it doesn't interfere with your concentration. The game, after all, is golf.

Obviously the problems of the swing vary with the player, so each jog must be personalized, but chances are good that none of them will have a very long shelf life anyway. As your game improves, some of your hesitant or half-forgotten routines will become reasonably well ingrained, so the need for that one particular jog will fade—only to be replaced by the need for another. It is Jack Nicklaus' contention that because there are so many little pieces of the swing to be remembered, the effort to recall each separate segment interferes with the next, so we should try to reduce the need for thinking and make everything as mechanical as possible. That's a philosophy that has a special appeal for me, as I suspect it does for most memory-impaired older golfers.

This procedure, incidentally, is hardly my own invention, nor is it limited to golf. Venus Williams, the world-class tennis professional and twice winner of the Wimbledon, has been observed studying her crib notes during the changeovers, mouthing reminders to herself to "Get under the ball" and "Bend your knees" and "Attack, attack, attack..."

Unfortunately, such are the shortcomings of a declining memory that I often forget for what each of the jog's letters stand or even forget to use the jog altogether. Nevertheless, because my muscles are blessed with a better memory than my head, the need for those little reminders has faded, although I'm still inclined to use them, if only occasionally and only after the fact. For example, there are about half a dozen small facets of my swing that occasionally elude me when I'm on the course. After several badly hit balls I'll analyze my swing, recognize that I had forgotten to perform one or two little motions—perhaps pivoting adequately or keeping my left arm stiff—and for the rest of that round I'll focus on "postscript" or <u>PS</u> for Pivot and Stiff. I realize that it's not a very profound recommendation, but it seems to work for me—at least somewhat and sometimes—so I mention it as a tool that *might* work as a short-term aid for *some* people *some* of the time.

5

PREPARING FOR ACTION

All right, so Big Blue, the IBM super-computer, *finally* managed to edge out Garry Kasparov in chess...but not until its second time around. And even then it took an army of human handlers, further assisted by a few temporary lapses on the part of Mr. Kasparov, for that collection of circuit-boards and electronic gadgetry to achieve its narrow victory.

Undeterred by the Big Blue victory, physiologists still insist on the superiority of the human brain over the complex circuitry of the computer board, a reassuring claim for senior golfers frustrated by the wide range of skills that must be meshed and memorized in order to master the myriad intricacies of the game. The many maneuvers and manipulations of golf are so broad and varied that most bewildered amateurs are convinced it takes more than just a single brain to store all its many details .

Considering the number and diversity of the demands of the game, it is not very surprising, then, that all the many details of the swing are not logically ordered and readily recalled. When on the practice range, therefore, it is important that you concentrate on just one piece of the swing at a time, understanding and adjusting the flaws in that piece that too often lead to poorly executed shots, and learning to groove and improve those other parts of the swing that help send the ball how and where you intend. Focus your concentration on just that one segment of the swing under consideration, hitting about a dozen balls in that mode, then going on to another element—repeating the routine and following the same procedure throughout the whole range of segments that constitutes the golf swing. The proper swing, after all, is a ritual sequence of movements that ideally and in time becomes rote, requiring neither thought nor analysis. The object is to learn and perfect the mechanics of each of those segments, engrave them into your muscle's memory banks, and finally to integrate them all into a perfect, natural swing that requires only minimal conscious thought for each application.

THE DANGERS OF INNOVATION

Unfortunately, the same inspired performance that seems to define us on the driving range often fails to accompany us onto the course. A fairly common cause of this disappointment is that we assume a level of muscle memory that is not yet really ours. That unwarranted glorification of skills that are really only partially developed encourages an inattention to some details that are critical to the proper execution of a good swing, resulting in serious damage to our style and our shot.

Such overconfidence and its disagreeable consequences is illustrated by the conceit once exhibited by Sarah, my wife's mother. Sarah was a remarkably good cook who had a special touch for making cakes and cookies. Unfortunately, she did like to improvise. I don't know how much of Sarah's talent was a naturally inherited skill and how much had been acquired while watching her mother cooking in the *shtetl* (the Russian village in which she lived) but by the time I came into the family her performance was very close to magical. Which is why I was so surprised when she once failed so dramatically with an award-winning recipe for cookies that had recently been published in one of the better women's magazines. They were not simply short of her standard—they were close to inedible.

"But ma," we asked, "did you follow the recipe?"
"Follow it?" she huffed. "I improved on it!"

By applying the lesson of Sarah's failure to our performance on the golf course, we should know not to try to improve while on the course whatever it was that worked well on the range. The special value of that constant practice on the range is in finally knowing from experience what shots we know we can play well, then playing them with confidence.

Frequent repetition of all the many small, complex pieces of the swing until they come together effectively and predictably is the best way to make them a natural and consistent part of your game, but blindly following the same routine without an understanding of the basis for the improved performance limits the value of the effort. It is important that you recognize what works in practice and understand *why* it works and make the necessary adjustments whenever the need becomes apparent. Eventually, you'll be able to hit with the confidence that you know *what* to do and *how* to do it and with the assurance that comes from having done it successfully many times before. By playing the shot you know from experience that you can play well, you can play it with confidence and consistency—which is ultimately the key to success on the course.

Incidentally, most of us like to use our time on the driving range as an opportunity to really swing that club and crush that ball, so the several woods and long irons become our weapons of choice during those practice sessions. As satisfying as that procedure may be at the moment, however, it could also be a major mistake. It is the *short* game, after all, that has the greatest impact on the score, and the *short* game that makes the money for us when settling our bets, but it is the short game to which we tend to give short shrift during our practice sessions on the range. Too many of us spend the bulk of our range time concentrating on our more dramatic, long-distance shots, thus feeding our egos but short-changing our potentially more profitable game nearer the green. Considering the value of the short game and the number of strokes it consumes (it is estimated that about 60 percent of all shots charged to our final score are taken within 100 yards of the green) such inattention is unwise and potentially expensive. Giving more time and attention to that otherwise neglected phase of the game is likely to provide a good chance of a major payoff later on.

As part of the training regimen, frequent and concentrated practice on the range has added value as an important role as a pregame warm-up. Whenever possible it is highly recommended that you spend at least 15 minutes on the range before teeing off, establishing the rhythm of your swing and reminding yourself of some of the basics you should be taking to the course. This advice is valid for all players, but it has special significance for older golfers who take a bit longer to get the blood flowing freely through less elastic veins.

In addition to the obvious value of committing to muscle memory the many details of a good swing, a major benefit to be derived from spending time on the range is psychological. The previous chapter made much of the importance of "confidence" as a fundamental ingredient of your game—a contention that bears repeating. With confidence in your swing, in your judgment for club selection, and in your ability to properly direct the ball toward its target, the likelihood of executing a smooth, powerful, and successful swing is vastly improved. Hitting well-struck ball after well-struck ball on the range can add enormously to your confidence in your ability to continue to do so at will—a state of mind that is probably the single most important ingredient in playing good golf. (On the other hand, of course, overconfidence can carry its own set of problems, such as the ill-chosen press on a hole you are unlikely to win—but that's grist for another mill.)

There is also a value in the adoption of a pre-stroke routine to help develop both concentration and confidence. That routine, intended to clear your head of the problems and emotions of a previously flawed shot, can be as foolish and trivial as touching the visor of your cap or taking one deep breath or wiggling your body or waggling your club—as long as it is precise and predictable Its purpose is simply to help you focus more completely on the task at hand and provide a mental and physical signal that the swing is now ready to begin. Incidentally, lest you think this is just another amateur's crutch, such a routine is practiced methodically by young professional hotshots and skilled amateurs alike. Mike Weir, the 2003 Master's winner in

Augusta, for example, invariably prepares for his attack with a preliminary half-backswing that brings the club parallel to the ground before
beginning over again in earnest—a ritual procedure that doesn't seem
to have hurt his game too much.

Much of this chapter has been spent on discussion of the practice range
as both a training field and as the site of a pregame warmup. This is the
proper moment, then, to introduce a note of caution into this illusion
of growing success. When I finally began to take the game of golf seriously I spent hours on the range polishing my skills and perfecting my
swing, an exercise that showcased me as one of the premier players of
the range. Unfortunately, that star-spangled pageant on the range was
not the end of the movie—merely its high point. I found that perfection on the range did not necessarily translate into adequacy on the
course. When practicing with an unlimited number of balls, one bad
shot would be followed by several follow-up attempts, during which
exercise I could determine the reason for the mishit and correct it.

The reality of life on the course, however, is an entirely different
milieu. Unlike swinging on the range, where repetition can reveal and
correct errors, a bad drive on the course is the end of the story for that
shot. Because the drive is followed by the use of a different club and
that club by still another club, there is little opportunity to effectively
analyze each individual problem and take advantage of the moment to
correct it.

The other, perhaps more relevant difference between range play and
attacking the course during a game is the level of confidence you bring
to the task. On the range you are fairly sure of what you are doing, or
are at least unconcerned about failure on any particular shot, and you
tend to swing with an easy rhythm that translates into a well-struck ball
with just the right loft and distance and grace. On the other hand,
when your partner or opponent is watching your next shot with anxiety and anticipation, you are more likely to tense up, grip too tightly,
swing too hard—and blow it. Of all Tom's many technical sugges-

tions, the most valuable for me, and I suspect of equal value for most other older students, is simply to *relax.*

This is not to demean the mechanical worth of all that practice. It is merely sage counsel to recognize the dichotomy between the pressures of play and the relaxed atmosphere of the driving range. During the game, where we may have part of our retirement savings on the line, we too easily forget some of the basics in order to over-concentrate on that one characteristic of great wood shots—distance! After all, having hit several dozen range balls straight and properly lofted, we obviously know what we're doing. Now, on the course, it seems to be time to skip to the next phase—time to unleash all our latent power and hit that ball a ton. Unfortunately, such striving too often comes at the expense of grace and rhythm. Replacing a six-inch divot or searching for the ball on a different fairway can be a costly and embarrassing road back to reality.

In short, practice on the range, while invaluable as a training proce-dure, does not necessarily yield results that can be repeated each time out. The caution, then, is to take your time when on the course, relax before each shot, then try to repeat the routine you had established and practiced successfully on the range. Afterward, particularly if the result was less than you had anticipated, analyze the details of the swing, try to ascertain just which bits of the procedure were at odds with your practice sessions, then concentrate on correcting the error the next time around. In time, the routine will become grooved and natural, but until then a good performance on the range, followed by an inadequate series of shots on the course, can be an agonizing source of frustration and anger—and a whole lot of self-pity.

6

THE BASIC GAME

Despite its apparent and puzzling complexity, Tom insists that golf is simply a judicious blending of the three basics: proper balance, timely hand release, and a firm left side. Bring them all together in just the right way and the game is a snap. That tends to sound a bit like enumerating the ancient list of the elements of nature as Fire, Water, Earth and Sky—it may be accurate as far as it goes, but it does seem to leave out a fair amount. He builds on that foundation by insisting that "golf is probably the only game in the world where every move that anybody has to make for a good golf swing is a natural move that the body wants to make anyway, and the only reason people have problems is that they have a tendency to restrict or exaggerate those moves." In other words, it's okay to think—just don't overdo it.

I have an ego problem accepting his theory that my body has better sense than my intellect, but I suspect he's right. On the other hand, inasmuch as the two of us (body and intellect) are consigned to working together, it makes little difference which of the two causes the problem—a bad swing leads to a bad shot.

Another Tomism is, "It matters little how fast or how slow you swing as long as all the proper factors are in place." That is obviously true, but for me the difficulty of getting all those "proper factors in place" is the root of the trouble. Each of the many pieces of the swing may be simple enough by itself, but it is putting all those pieces together as a comprehensible whole that tends to boggle the mind and inflate the score.

His advice is to concentrate on each of the few essential components of the game, adjust them according to the limitations of age and flexibility, then practice each until it becomes automatic. It is then simply a matter of blending them into a single uniform motion to achieve the perfect swing. My problem is that trying to remember and identify all the many and complex component parts of a good golf swing is almost enough to drive me back to the gin table, so I gratefully accept his efforts toward simplification and try to keep my mind on just his three fundamentals:

- Balance

- Hand release

- Firm left side

All the rest of golf's disciplines, he says, simply feed those three basics. Taking each in its turn:

BALANCE

Perhaps the most important basic feature of a good swing, for both consistency and control, is the maintenance of proper balance. An imbalance during the swing almost guarantees a misdirected hit or a serious loss of distance and very probably both. Inadequately understood is the fact that the head controls most of the weight and balance of the body, so first among Tom's list of inviolable commandments (a list more numerous than the biblical ten, if a bit less consequential) is that the head *must not move* during the swing (no doubt a doctrine reinforced by the childhood memory of the golf swing experiment in his garage).

To better understand the impact of imbalance during the swing try adopting a drill commonly used by most pros: swing the club while standing erect, keeping your head still and feet almost touching. Then repeat the exercise after moving your head ever so slightly to either side. The changing weight of the swing will likely throw you seriously off balance. By keeping your head still and pivoting from the lower part of your body you will probably remain steady and more in control. If you are able to maintain a good balance while keeping your feet together on the practice range, it should be a snap when you employ the same rhythm using the proper stance on the course.

To gain a better understanding of the role the weight shift plays in the body's balance, try swinging the club with your feet very close together, but keeping your head stabilized. Then do the same thing, but move your head slightly—and be prepared to fall.

Despite the common admonition not to take your eyes off the ball, it is the *head*—not the face—that is the determining factor in maintaining balance. The eyes can move, the face can move—just *don't move the head*, either from side-to-side or by changing its elevation. On the other hand, permission for me to move my face may not be such a benign option. I don't know whether it stemmed from impatience or from an unquenchable curiosity, but one of my game's more serious problems had been my anxiety to observe the results of each swing at the ball. In order to see where my drive was going or to determine how well it was hit or even to assess the progress of my short chip or putt, I was too often tempted to sneak a peek to check the results, which in turn caused my head to move, which in turn disrupted the intended point of contact of the clubhead with the ball. It was a hard lesson to learn, but I now concentrate on keeping my head *and face* perfectly still throughout the swing and my eyes firmly focused on the spot where the ball had been before its contact with the clubface.

An addendum to the instructions limiting movement of the head is the matter of transferring weight to the right side during the backswing. Although a small transfer of weight during the swing is reasonable and inevitable, quantifying the precise degree of that transfer—such as X percent on the backswing, then Y percent on the follow-through—is obviously folly. By keeping the head perfectly still, however, with neither lateral sway nor changes in its elevation, the proper proportion of the weight transfer is a natural phenomenon that requires neither thought nor manipulation, simply occurring automatically. (Much, perhaps even most of this movement is controlled by the performance of the "pivot," a move that will be analyzed in detail in Chapter 7, "The Swinging Game.")

Meanwhile, all of these factors—the balance, the head movement, the weight transfer—are impacted by the *stance*, the very first decision a golfer must make when standing up to the ball. That's a big responsibility so early in the game: where to place the ball in relation to the feet; how great a reach toward the ball you program into the stance; how far apart you place your feet, even how to stand. Fortunately, as with everything else in golf, the rules governing the details of the swing are individualized and flexible, so you have some room for personalizing your preferences. The relevant factors include your innate hand/eye coordination, your natural sense of balance, the style of your swing and a few other such variables. Because each of these maneuvers is determined at least somewhat by the style, strength and flexibility of each player, the rules regarding stance are a bit less than hard and fast, but there are a few useful guidelines that should be considered and tried.

The first important item to recognize seems fairly obvious: for maximum propulsion you need the most solid contact possible between the clubhead and the ball. The integrity of that contact is largely a reflection of your ability to locate the absolute bottom point of the downswing, which in turn is dependent on the nature of the swing and the arc of the clubhead in motion. The problem, as we'll see later, is that because of the individuality of styles associated with each person's swing, no universal stance or ball placement can fit all players, so we must each discover our own best approach.

There are as many preferences for the proper stance as there are golf instructors to suggest them. The most common recommendation is to stand with the ball just inside the left heel when using the driver, then sliding the ball increasingly toward the center of your stance for each successively shorter club until you wind up with the ball in the middle of your stance for the wedge. The rationale for this stance is that the goal of shorter clubs is generally to achieve greater loft, and that bringing the club-head down into the ball earlier more effectively encourages that loft. There is logic to that presumption, but there is some question of just how rigidly those instructions should be followed. There is the law of physics that suggests keeping the ball closer to your left heel in order to catch the ball on the upswing, thereby giving it more loft, but you might also achieve the same goal by hitting the ball earlier with a more open clubface. It is advisable, therefore, to find your own best position for the ball's placement by swinging the various clubs over an empty patch of grass without the presence of the ball, watching where the clubhead hits the grass with fair consistency and then accepting that spot as the proper ball placement for you. The width of the stance is important to help stabilize balance, but be careful not to overdo it. A stance too wide reduces control of the hip and leg motions, thereby restricting the flexibility needed for a good swing.

Another valuable recommendation is a stance intended to help flatten the swing in order to ensure a more solid contact with the ball. Position your body's center slightly to the right of the ball at address, so that a vertical line drawn downward from your head would end several inches to the right of the ball on the ground. This right-oriented stance causes the right shoulder to drop several inches below the level of the left shoulder, giving the appearance of a body positioned to explode toward the target. That posture helps promote the right hand as the generator of power and reduces the role of the left hand, a very profitable division of labor when searching for maximum impact.

Posture, too, can play a valuable role in the consistency of the swing. For maximum control of the path of the clubhead during the swing, stand straight, bending only from the waist rather than from the shoulder, avoiding the forward curve of the body associated with the stance of the aged. For your woods and longer irons, spread your feet apart about the width of your shoulders, keeping your weight just a bit more centered on the soles of your feet than on the heels, but in all cases *stand straight and bend from the waist.*

Of critical importance, too, for an efficient strike, is the distance you stand from the ball and the posture you assume during the address. If you stand too close or if your knees are bent too much, the clubhead may dig into the dirt behind the ball with potentially disastrous results. Inasmuch as scientific accuracy in measuring the proper distance is unlikely (the use of a tape measure before every swing will not endear you to the rest of your foursome) my personal preference is to stand with knees stiff and with the far edge of the clubhead barely reaching the ball. Then, when I bend my knees slightly, I find the distance just about right. When in doubt, however, standing a little too far from the ball is better than just a bit too close. Even when standing too far you are unlikely to miss the ball altogether, but standing too close could very easily result in slamming the clubhead into the ground just before contact—a fairly common and very embarrassing mishap.

THE HANDS

Most of us become so committed to certain characteristics of our swing—really hard for power or extra slow for control or with an exaggerated pivot or a severely limited takeaway, or whatever—that we pay inadequate attention to the role of the hands in the whole affair. The limitations of age tend to restrict the effective range of some of our options, so we should concentrate on using that which is available to us, but using it with greater efficiency. The more effective use of the hands is one of the primary keys to more powerful and better controlled golf and is independent of the size or strength of the player, so that is a good place to start.

Beyond the broad issue of "Hand Release" as one of Tom's three basics, his interpretation of the specific roles of the hands are worth examination:

> 1—Both hands have roles to play in grasping and swinging the club, but because most power is generated by action of the right hand Tom suggests using a firmer grip and a greater emphasis on the right hand during the downswing.
>
> By way of illustration, he likes to use the example of trying to move a stalled car, insisting that we don't pull the car to get it moving, but push it for maximum utilization of our full power. Concentrating our power in our left hand during a golf swing has the effect of pulling the club down and toward the target, which is a motion that does not generate very much force By fixing the emphasis on the right hand when coming into the ball we are essentially pushing the clubhead and ball toward that target, thus providing the stroke with very much more authority. An added benefit to this procedure, by the way, is that it helps encourage a more

concerted follow-through, thereby adding considerable control to the direction of the flight of the ball.

2—There are almost as many recommendations for the proper grip as there are people to teach them, but the safest rule is to stay with what feels most comfortable, with a single exception: grip the club firmly and mostly with the right hand, but do not squeeze. The determination of most amateurs to reach the green in two on a long par-four tends to encourage a "death grip" and there's already enough tension in the game without seeking ways to instill more. Tension is one of the greatest enemies of good golf, and a body already reduced by age really doesn't need the further limitations of tightened muscles and lost rhythm. The game, after all, especially for older players, is not about strength but about rhythm, timing, and consistency. We are much more likely to achieve extra distance by the timely snap of the wrist at the moment of impact than by a body slam.

An important adjunct to this advice is to keep the left hand grip light and relaxed by limiting the grasp of the club to just the last several fingers of the hand rather than holding it in the palm. The natural inclination is to apply more muscle for more power in order to move the ball a greater distance, but it just doesn't work that way. Instead of trying to kill the ball with high speed and flexed muscle, a greater reliance on the rhythm of the swing will put you well ahead of the game and further down the fairway. Once again, it's the snap of the wrist at the moment of impact that provides the greatest power, so whatever maneuver increases the vigor of that snap is the one most likely to add distance to your game.

Another recommendation for increasing the acceleration of that wrist snap is to concentrate the pressure of the thumb and forefinger of your right hand while still relaxing your left hand. That helps ease those muscles of hands otherwise tensed by the tight grip, thereby encouraging a much more powerful ball-strike.

More than incidentally, another enemy of a well-timed snap of the wrist is a tendency to cock our hands ahead of the ball at the set-up or to break them at the start of the takeaway. We should keep our hands roughly over the ball at the set-up, avoiding the natural inclination to cock them ahead of the ball, and keep them unbroken at least until the early stage of the backswing. It is the violent snap of wrists unhinging at the moment of contact of the clubhead with the ball that is necessary to achieve adequate power for a good golf shot, and the slowed reflexes of seniors may hinder our ability to bring previously cocked wrists back into play in time for maximum impact.

At the setup, relax both the muscles and the mind, avoiding the perils of a "death grip" that could destroy the necessary rhythm of a good swing...Keep your hands roughly over the ball, avoiding the natural inclination to cock them too far forward.

HAND RELEASE

It may be obvious that the speed of the clubhead at the moment of impact will determine the distance of the ball's flight, but how to achieve maximum speed at that point is a bit less obvious. As noted earlier, our inclination is to swing faster in order to hit harder, but the fact is that arm-speed during the downswing plays a relatively minor role in the speed of the clubhead. Then, because that previous hard swing didn't achieve the results we had intended, we try to make up for that ungained yardage by increasing the clubhead speed even more for the next shot, swinging even harder, which in turn throws our balance, our rhythm, and our control completely out of whack. And so our downward spiral into depression takes root.

A much more effective increase in the velocity of the clubhead may be achieved by sharply breaking the wrists at about the moment of the clubhead's contact with the ball. The action of that break moves the clubhead at a much higher rate of speed than can possibly be accomplished by pulling the club back down to the ball, however much strength you might bring to the task. If converted into geometric terms, for example, the wrists are closer to the center of a circle, while the clubhead marks the outer rim of that circle. Those few inches of rapid movement of the wrists, therefore, translate into a very fast speeding clubhead at the perimeter of that circle, so although increasing the speed of the arms during the downswing phase may seem like the prelude to power, that increased velocity pales by comparison to the clubhead speed generated by the snap of the wrists.

It is undeniably good to be strong, but it is more the timing and the rhythm of the swing than the speed and power of the downswing motion that makes the difference in the flight of the ball, a very reassuring revelation for we older golfers. One example of that axiom is Margaret Dewberry, a 90-year-old grandmother who recently shot a score of ninety at the Forest Hills Golf Course in Augusta, Georgia. But don't stop there. Barrett Nichols of The Meadows Country Club in Sarasota, Florida, last year shot a score of 92—pretty good for a guy who at the time was 100 years old. (For some of us, that goal of shooting our age holds the very attractive promise of living a very long life indeed.)

FIRM LEFT SIDE

I know that aging has changed me at least somewhat. I like to think that it has left me just a bit wiser and maybe slightly improved in other ways as well, but mostly I'm just balder, shorter, and weaker. I can live with bald and I've never been very tall, but it's "weak" that hurts my ego. Throughout this book you will be told that it's the short game that's reflected on the winning scorecard, that it's the chip and the pitch and the putt that really count...and that's true. But it is also true—despite my remonstrations against trying to crunch the ball into oblivion—that it is the thrill of a long, high, hard drive that keeps bringing us back to the course week after frustrating week.

So now for a little more of Tom's advice on power hitting. According to Tom, one of the single most important factors in gaining real distance from a golf ball is properly firming up the left side when swinging through the ball. He asks that you visualize a whip in your hand. In order to get the whip to "crack" when you swing it hard, you must snap your wrist so the handle and its adjoining section come to a sharp stop, while the far end section of the whip continues its forward motion. If both the handle and the arm continue to fly in the same direction without that sharp interruption in its forward motion, there will be no crack at the end.

Much the same condition attends the swinging of the club. A search for power utilizes the entire body—arms, legs, and torso. When your body's coil has begun to reverse itself and your arms and club are coming down full steam from the top of your backswing, the theory of the whip-snap demands a stopping point for some of that action. If the rest of your body follows the club's forward motion beyond its moment of contact with the ball there will be no "crack" at the end of the swing. By rotating your hip and keeping your left knee straight after you hit the ball, your arms and club will continue their heady journey toward the hole, the wrists will break naturally, and that critical snap will occur.

An assist to that recommendation is the advice to pause at the top of the backswing, a brief delay that encourages the rest of the body (notably the hips) to start moving toward the target slightly in advance of the club. One way to achieve that pause is at what seems to be the end of the backswing, force the clubhead backward just a little more. That extra move seems to serve as a natural pause during which the rest of the body starts its motion in advance of the arms and club. I know that it's better to be big and strong and coordinated, but sometimes you just have to work with what you've got

7

THE SWINGING GAME

In the early 1940s, when I was first hypnotized by the captivating beat of jazz, I remember hearing that "It don't mean a thing if you ain't got that swing…(doo-wah, doo-wah)." I believed it then and I believe it now, but its application for me has shifted a bit—from a toe-tapping rhythm to the principles of golf.

The swing is the cornerstone of the entire game of golf, the fundamental action that guides every club for just about every shot. Nevertheless, the swing itself is not a single, independent activity. It is simply the genre in which a number of other individual pieces of performance congregate.

A good swing is a collection of interrelated segments, each impacting on the others. It may be evident, for example, that the shot that just went bad was the consequence of an inadequate pivot, and so you assume a good pivot must be the key to everything. Trouble is, the next shot enjoyed a perfect pivot but your right elbow flew away from your body on the takeaway, so the ball went…wherever.

Serious improvement in your game requires a judicious blending of those individual parts into a single workable whole—all of which taken together comprise the swinging game.

The previous chapter focused on some of Tom's basic golf principles, but even a category as narrowly defined as that does not necessarily end there. As in cooking, although the right ingredients in the right amounts are all essential to a quality product, the temperature and cooking time and a host of other details can still make the difference between delicacy and disaster. Whatever the specifics of grip and stance and weight shift, there still remains the broader outline into which Tom's basics must fit—that is, the style and grace of the swing itself.

And that's not easy. The complexity of the problem is best understood in mathematical terms: In a circle defined by a six-and-one-half foot radius (that's roughly two-and-one-half feet of arm connected to about four feet of club), after the clubhead leaves its starting point it must swing along 40 feet of circumference (about 20 feet of takeaway, then 20 feet of return) before bringing that one square inch of the clubface's sweet spot back to the same little one-and-one-half-inch ball it had left moments earlier. Given these conditions, if the likelihood of making proper contact seems like a theoretical impossibility, my several decades of trying unsuccessfully to meet that goal provides a solid foundation for such skepticism. On the other hand, there is enough evidence that others, less deserving than ourselves and without the advantage of our new titanium clubheads and graphite shafts, have already succeeded, so we should stifle our pessimism and keep on trying.

All of which helps justify one of the more important cautions in the game of golf: don't over-swing! Just take it easy, concentrating more on the rhythm of the swing than on its impact with the ball, and you'll be way ahead of the game. Meanwhile, the three major components of the total swing to be discussed here, each in its turn, are the backswing with its takeaway, the downswing, and the follow-through.

THE BACKSWING

The backswing serves a more complex purpose than simply getting the club high enough to come crashing back down through the ball. The whole procedure of the takeaway and backswing is one of the most important phases of the entire swing, so a solid grasp of the nuances of the process is more likely to make the difference between a triumphal march home and sneaking in through the back door.

First, when starting the backswing keep the mind and body relaxed and concentrate on those key procedures necessary for making good contact with the ball. We are often so anxious to "get to it already" that we tend to fixate on the anticipated results rather than on the best means of achieving them. One way to ease the body's tension and encourage a fluid rhythm is to devise a simple and continuing routine, a "trigger" to get the blood flowing and all the processes started. As one of many possible triggers Tom recommends the "grip press" (as distinct from the "forward press," which is a cocking of the hands ahead of the ball, a technique more appropriate for chip shots close to the green). When fully prepared to start the takeaway but prior to any actual movement, just grip the club a little more firmly with the right hand while relaxing the grip of the left hand. The point is to use this action as a subconscious reminder of the details of the ritual that should then come into play for a consistently solid contact with the ball at the end of the swing.

There is, of course, no limit to the number or variety of triggers that may be employed, simply whatever feels most comfortable and works most reliably. The object, after all, is merely to establish a relaxed state of concentration and a routine that may help initiate a spontaneous series of movements necessary for a good golf swing, a routine which in turn may be structured according to each player's individual needs and style.

"Keep your eye on the ball" is another reasonable suggestion to help find that state of relaxed concentration, but the command has become such a cliché that it no longer has impact as significant technical advice—the words are there and the admonition is valid, but its meaning no longer registers. Essentially, keeping your eye on the ball is all about concentration and focus.

At about the time of set-up and before starting the swing, twist your head slightly to the right, just far enough so that at the end you find yourself peering down on the ball a bit more with your left eye than evenly with both. That action and the hesitation that precedes it seem to serve several functions: first, as a moment of contemplation, easing the transition from a static state to a smooth and graceful swinging motion and second is its benefit as a backswing trigger. I find that twisting my head slightly to the right and freezing the focus of my left eye on the ball encourages my concentration on the task at hand and helps stabilize my head, preventing me from swaying during the back-swing (a remedy comparable to Tom's childhood experience of locking his head into the vise of two-by-fours, but without its painful side effects.)

Another way to "keep your eye on the ball" derives from the way you position the ball on the tee. Most people keep their eye on the top of the ball as they peer down on it from above, but by placing the ball so the maker's name or other marking is on its right-hand side as the target for the clubhead it is easier to concentrate your focus on that mark throughout the swing.

The style and tempo with which you pull the club back sets the pat-tern for all that ensues, so the various elements of the procedure should be understood and exercised with all possible care and consistency. Some professional golfers, who tend to be a bit younger and a lot more limber than most readers of this book, begin their backswing with a slight movement of the hip in order to set their swing in motion, but many older golfers have trouble bringing all their limbs into proper sync in a timely fashion. A highly recommended alternative, then, is to start your turn with an absolutely united front, simultaneously engag-ing all the movable parts of the body that are to be used in that swing—hips, hands, arms, and shoulders. Forcing the hips to remain part of that introductory action rather than acting on their own encourages a unified response by the otherwise independent members of the upper body. Without that restriction, it is more likely that the arms will move back into swinging position ahead of time, very possi-bly resulting in a sway of the body that will disrupt the proper path of the club when it tries to return to the ball—and that's how divots are born.

And then there is the pivot!

Pending contrary evidence from experiments in human cloning, no two of us are exactly alike. Our golf-related strengths and flaws and overall styles, for example, vary from player to player as predictably as do our personalities, which means, of course, that no one set of instructions fits all. The one debilitating defect that is the downfall of one golfer may have little or no impact on the next, so the solutions must be as individually styled as are the shortcomings, but for many—perhaps most—senior amateurs that keystone defect is the pivot. An improper or inadequate swivel during the take-away is generally the cause of more grief and more strokes than most any other part of their game. Inadequately executed, the pivot can seriously compromise the necessary rhythm and balance of the swing by interfering with some of its subsequent segments, thereby making solid contact with the ball much less likely. During the backswing, for example, it is important to keep most of the body centered over the ball, coiled around an imaginary rod running through the center of the body. It is all right to transfer some weight from left to right so that when the turn is complete a slightly greater percentage of the body's weight is on the inside edge of the right foot, but your head should remain directly over the ball, with your face peering straight down at it over your left shoulder. An incomplete pivot, however, changes the position and weight distribution of your body when returning to the ball, so that instead of being directly over it at the end of the takeaway, the club and the weight of your body are now behind the ball with the body balanced unevenly on the outside edge of the right foot, unfortunately making a deeply dug divot at the end of the downswing a highly likely possibility.

In order to better understand the nature and feel of the maneuver, Tom recommends a simple exercise. Prepare for the start of the swing, then imagine someone behind your right shoulder calling your name. Chances are that in order to see who it is, you will turn from the waist to face him, without laterally moving your head. By making the turn in this way your body will remain properly balanced, your head will not have moved, either laterally or in elevation, and the transfer of your weight will have been properly proportioned. In addition, I find that by tightening those muscles of my upper left arm and shoulder during the turn I can more readily force my body into a tighter coil which then unleashes itself into a more explosive release when it comes time to strike the ball.

In order to better understand the proper motion of a good pivot, get set up and prepared to swing the club, then imagine someone behind your right shoulder calling your name.

The natural inclination of such a move is to turn from the waist to face the questioner without laterally moving your head. This motion will help assure that the body remains propberly balanced.

Revision time. A few pages back I examined the procedures initiating the backswing and concluded (or agreed with the conclusion of those who really know) that the proper and necessary technique to insure grace and continuity in that segment of the swing is to start your turn with an "absolutely united front, simultaneously engaging all the movable parts of the body that are to be used in that swing—hips, hands, arms, and shoulders." That may well be true generally, but as Tom insists, there are almost no absolutes in golf and this directive is no different, so I take this opportunity to reconsider and recant. I recently went to Tom, traumatized by my too frequent tendency to hit the ball to the right and/or dig into the turf behind the ball when coming back down from on high. Both problems, he insisted, were related to the way I began my takeaway. He noted that after starting my turn my left knee continued to face more outward than around and to the right, so he advised me to start my backswing by rolling my left knee around more in the manner of a pivot. I now use the twist of that knee as a trigger for the start of the takeaway, slightly in advance of the rest of my body—and my future looks bright once again. A slightly premature movement of just one knee may not be quite the same as simultaneous, but if sins come in gradations, this is a very small one indeed.

A large part of the reason for all this emphasis on the pivot is to help your body "coil" adequately in order to provide the maximum available power when you unwind, which is a primary goal of most golf instruction books. They point out that when a tightly coiled body unwinds it can add as many as thirty yards to a 240 yard drive. Very good, but at our age few of us are able to reach the initial 240 yards with anything less than a small-bore canon anyhow, so fantasizing about the best way to reach 270 yards on a drive is like dreaming of ways to spend our lottery winnings.

Nevertheless, however difficult it may be for some seniors to achieve a maximum coil, it is a goal worth pursuing—but only within the limits of our natural capabilities. If we push it too far outside our comfort zone the effort could cause more damage to our swing than it may be worth. Even more than the power, after all, it is the fluidity and tempo of the swing that count. The number and variety of procedures to be incorporated in a well executed swing requires that we keep them all as simple and uniform as possible.

In order to keep to a minimum the confusion of what to do with what part of our body and when, we should limit the variables of the swing as much as we reasonably can. Accordingly, every effort must be made to maintain maximum consistency in the details of the club's takeaway so the same route can be followed during its downswing phase. If, for example, we keep our left arm and elbow straight on both takeaway and downswing and at the start of the follow-through, the arm and club tend to take on the more dependable characteristics of a pendulum. Such a procedure minimizes erratic changes in the swing path, increasing the likelihood of returning the clubhead to the ball at a position very nearly the same as that from which it started. (In similar fashion, I find that I best keep my left arm uniformly straight by keeping my left elbow locked and rigid.) It helps, too, to keep the right elbow tucked into the waist until that point when any further turning of the torso forces their separation. If all this is done according to the book—stretching the arms back and around on the takeaway, keeping the left arm firm, and pivoting fully and properly—it should all combine to force the left shoulder under the chin, thereby giving us enough body coil to produce the controlled power we seek. I might add, too, that a smooth continuity is aided by sliding the clubhead back low to the ground during the early part of the takeaway, not lifting it until it starts the later part of its journey around the body.

The left arm should be kept firm and straight throughout the entire backswing and well into the early stages of the follow-through, until the continuing mechanics of the swing finally forces it to bend.

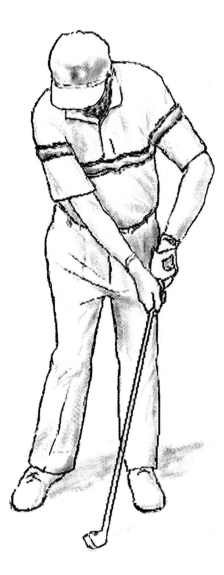

Relaxing the locked position of the left elbow prematurely seriously limits the power you can bring to the impact of the clubhead on the ball, greatly reducing both the control and the distance of its flight.

EVEN THE MOST RIGID RULES ARE FLEXIBLE

Tom's insistence on keeping the left arm straight throughout the swing is unassailable, but is also at odds with his philosophy that there is no absolutely right or wrong way to swing a club, that whatever works for you is the right way to go. That inconsistency was highlighted by the remarkable example of one of Tom's very good friends, the late Ed Furgol, whose left arm was badly damaged and permanently deformed as the result of a childhood accident. Poor kid. He didn't know that because he was unable to keep a straight left arm during the takeaway and follow-through he would be unable to play really good golf, so in his ignorance he went on to win the United States Open in 1954. So much for inviolable absolutes. The fact is, of course, that what may be right for the bulk of mankind is not necessarily good for each of its individual members.

Tom insists that it matters little how fast or how slowly you swing the club, the important thing is simply to get it to the proper place at the proper time. His concern is that a consciously slow swing may make us more tense and thereby corrupt the integrity of our rhythm and disrupt our timing. For some of us, however, the more considered motion of the slower swing enables us to achieve greater control and—once again, as Tom says—if it works for you, it's right for you. Accordingly, I have taken a page from Jack Nicklaus' book. He agrees with Tom that we must each be true to our own unique style, in this instance comparing his own more deliberative method to the quicker motions of the four-time Masters winner, Arnie Palmer. For the first twelve inches of his backswing Nicklaus takes the club back at an abnormally slow pace, a procedure that seems to work for me as well, albeit at a rather different level of result. It allows me to establish my tempo at the right pace and helps set the tone for the balance of the swing, somehow discouraging me from rushing it at a later, more critical stage in the process.

One of the troubles with aging (that is, besides arthritic joints, diminished eyesight, failing memory, etc.) is that we lose our flexibility, so

when we try too hard to generate a full swing we are faced with a pair
of problems: first, the exaggerated swing forces us to roll back on our
heels, and secondly, our head is likely to raise up. Remember that we
have that six and one-half-foot stretch of arm and club and those myriad variables that define the swing, so under the best of circumstances
the likelihood of coming back to exactly the same spot from which we
took off is pretty limited. When we add to that the extra variations of a
body that has moved and of an arc different from that plotted by the
backswing, the odds of reaching the starting point with the clubhead
properly positioned can become astronomical. In which case, according to Tom…then don't! Just don't try to bring the club back that far.
He says we should learn to be content with what we have rather than
engage in a futile struggle for something clearly outside our range of
abilities (which is also a pretty good mantra for our life outside of golf).
We should concentrate on staying within our "comfort zone," that area
of the game in which we can perform without undue strain or stress. If
we can no longer follow through as far as we could in the past or as far
as we think we should, okay, then we shouldn't try. If the club can only
move up to the right shoulder on the backswing and around to the left
shoulder on the follow-through, that's good enough. Don't make
demands on muscles that cannot be fulfilled. By forcing them to work
outside of their "comfort zone," you are more likely to sway or change
elevation, thereby losing both power and control. The only truly
important distance for the club to travel, after all, is contained in those
few inches before and after its impact with the ball, so there is no particular advantage in exchanging moderate distance and good control
for a mishit and misery.

THE DOWNSWING

Now, having finished all those lengthy and complex manipulations of
the takeaway, it's finally time to bring the club back down from its hes-

itant perch at the top of the backswing and to revel in the thrilling climax to this whole drama—the explosive smash of clubhead into ball.

Well, relax. It doesn't quite work that way. In reality, the downswing is little more than the culmination of all those preliminaries, just another moment in a continuum that simply blends all the separate elements of the total swing into a single rhythmic motion. If all those independent details were properly developed and integrated—the rhythm and the tempo and the rigid left arm and the tight pivot and the controlled right elbow, etc.—the path and performance of the downswing have already been programmed and the results effectively preordained. Very simply, the quality of the downswing largely reflects the integrity of the backswing, and giving in to a thirst for the drama of an explosive blast can do little more than derail the whole process. The results depend not on the power and the speed of the downward motion of the club preliminary to hitting the ball, but on the harmonious interaction of all the individual segments that make up the whole. That may not be true for your teenage grandchild, but senior golfers with limited experience and skill must rely on rhythm much more than on displays of power to compete effectively in the world of senior amateur golf.

In brief, Tom and his fellow professionals can throw everything they've got into a mighty clout and then watch as their ball flies straight off into the sunset, but the rest of us had better proceed with a lot more patience and restraint. Using the performance of the pros as no more than an outline for our own impossible dream, we should simply concentrate on the basic elements of a good golf swing, then apply that style and technique to our own game within our own limitations, focusing specifically on:

- the tempo and basic characteristics of the swing
- the firming up of the left side
- the fact and the nature of the follow-through

THE TEMPO

Earlier, I referred to Tom's disinterest in the speed of the swing, whether fast or slow, just as long as it remains smooth and consistent and returns to the same point from which it started. I, however, cannot be quite that casual about the trip back down from its apex. For me to maximize the reduced power and effectuate the limited hand/eye coordination my aging muscles are able to bring to the swing I, as do most senior amateur golfers, require a bit more time. For example, if my hands are properly cocked at the top of the backswing, by bringing the club back down to the ball too swiftly it is likely that my hands will remain ahead of the clubhead by the time it returns to the ball, in which case the open clubface will send the ball flying sharply off to the right—and into the woods or lake or history.

It's obvious that the increased speed of a club during the downswing, properly controlled, can add many yards to the flight of the ball, but "properly controlled" is not necessarily a given as descriptive of the swing of most seniors. We simply need more time to coordinate our thoughts and our muscles than a hell-bent downswing will allow. A determination to hit that ball a country mile feeds our dreams, but ultimately does little to help our game. The reality, of course, is that aside from a few truly powerful (and young) professionals like John Daly, whose average drive is very close to 300 yards, for most of us it's the rhythm and the timing of the swing and the accuracy of the contact with the ball that is going to be most effective in propelling it toward its goal and reducing our score.

The impediment to a carefully considered swing has much to do with the macho sense of power that attaches to wrapping the club around the neck on the backswing, then coming back down to the ball with all the strength we can muster. As was noted earlier, most of the distance and direction of the flight of the ball is determined by those few inches of swing before and after the clubhead meets the ball so, at least at our level of strength and expertise, much of the rest of that swing is simply wasted. That point was raised in the last chapter, but a special emphasis on the first few inches after impact deserves some further discussion. Two-time winner of the United States Open, Julius Boros, used the expression "collect the ball" and that probably says it best. Don't just hit the ball, but try to have the clubhead merge with it, if just for a nanosecond. It is certainly true that by keeping the ball and clubhead together, however briefly, helps greatly in controlling the direction of the flight of the ball, but there is another significant value to that brief marriage: It is not just the smack of the clubhead that propels the ball—it is the power generated by the compression of the ball, achieved and released at the moment of impact, that has the greater effect. That compression of the ball when it meets the clubhead concentrates an energy that helps immeasurably in adding distance to its flight, in much the same fashion and according to the same principle that recognizes the extra thrust gained from the appropriate snap of the wrists. (The physics of compression will be discussed in greater detail in Chapter 19, "The Equipment.") Even more valuable for me, however, has been the awareness of the many benefits that accrue from simply staying with the ball as long as possible, adding as it does to the rhythm and tempo of my total swing.

KEEP A FIRM LEFT SIDE

Chapter 6, "The Basic Game," spoke of the importance of firming up the left side in order to achieve maximum distance, a process that depends on instituting a slight turn of the hips just before the start of the downswing—not necessarily the easiest of maneuvers. In theory and in time that move should become automatic and properly integrated into the full pattern of the downswing, but until that magical moment we can use all the help we can get. What works for me is using that pause between the end of my backswing and just prior to the start of my downswing to add a slight extra twist to my coil, bringing the clubhead just a bit further back and my left shoulder just a little more tightly tucked under my chin. The natural counteraction to that effort is to start my hip's rotation, which in turn triggers the unwinding action and brings all the subsequent motions into their properly positioned and precisely timed sequences.

There are many maneuvers of considerable value in generating power, but two that share the spotlight also share the same moment of activity: the transition from the conclusion of the backswing to the start of the downswing. The first piece of that duo is the pivot (covered in much greater detail later) which is best achieved by having completed your backswing with your back facing directly toward the target. Such a concluding posture guarantees that your pivot was both full and complete and that you had probably avoided any damaging weight shift to the right.

For me, a very productive partner to that pivot is a momentary pause during the period of transition. That brief inaction has value as a trigger to the preliminary turn of the hips, which serves to firm up the left side and helps stabilize my body, helping minimize the dangers from an unwanted and unanticipated sway.

THE FOLLOW-THROUGH

Now comes the moment of truth. Whether yours is the full and vigorous swing of youth or the more gentle, restricted swing of non-athletes past their prime, the last segment in this series of moves remains the same—the necessity to follow through after you strike the ball. More than almost any other aspect of your swing, the follow-through is what helps provide distance and achieve control over direction. The importance of a full and conscientious follow-through, incidentally, is hardly limited to fairway shots, but is an equally important factor in pitching and chipping and blasting out of traps. It is simply a basic and essential part of a good golf swing.

During several of the preceding paragraphs I referred to the general benefits I found in a slowed swing. They are worth repeating now, but with a somewhat revised emphasis. A younger body can achieve a tight coil, bringing the club all the way back around the head, then all the way through the ball and around to the other side of the head on the follow-through—and still go dancing that same night. Some of us past middle-age are a bit more constricted in our swing, however, and must depend more on subtlety than on brute force in order to power the ball any distance. As was mentioned a few pages earlier, most of the real force of the swing is generated by that handful of inches before and after the clubhead's contact with the ball. The older golfer, then, should reduce his dependence on the overall speed and power of the total swing, concentrating instead on finesse and on the efficient use of those pieces of the swing that are solidly under his control.

By examining the swing in its entirety it becomes evident that the most important portion is that segment that begins with the snap at the point of contact with the ball, then continues with the acceleration from that point onward. A somewhat slowed return from the peak of the backswing makes it easier to achieve that critical acceleration through the ball, the explosion referred to earlier.

An added advantage of the reduced club speed is that it provides us more time to think about some of the other requirements for a good swing and to bring some of those details under control. The point is that the dynamics of a good swing extend well beyond the drama of the clubhead striking the ball. It is at the moment of contact, when the ball actually lays on the face of the club gathering steam during that instant of compression and expansion (more on this in Chapter 19), that the power of the stroke is determined. By increasing the speed of your club during its downswing phase it is even less likely that you will sufficiently increase the power of the clubhead at that moment of impact with the ball, which after all is the critical moment to reap the full benefit of that speed.

Tom's very insistent advice, referred to earlier, is that at the top of the backswing your back should be facing the target. Then, at the end of the follow-through it's your chest and the grip-end of the club should be aimed in that direction. At the conclusion of the swing the bulk of your weight should favor your left side, the success of which can be measured by the fact of finishing your pivot on the toe of your right foot. Additionally, the left arm should remain straight for as long as comfortable after hitting the ball, a move which encourages the whole body to aim toward the target, lending additional power and control to the exercise.

Considering all the demands made on the minds and movements of the older golfer during the swinging action, it's hardly surprising that so many recommended procedures go unfulfilled. The benefit of delaying some of that action by reducing the speed of the club and pausing at the top of the backswing is to enable us, for however brief a respite, to more calmly consider what we're supposed to do next and to meet that requirement with a somewhat greater degree of control. For example a narrow focus on correcting the perils of our flying right elbow (i.e., pointing the elbow toward the horizon rather than to the ground during the backswing) is likely to divert our attention away our pivot, or cause us to forget about uncocking our wrists in a timely fashion.

Unfortunately, there is no easy answer to this problem of having too much to remember except to remember it in our subconscious. Slowing everything down does help, but that is still not enough. The best solution is to practice each maneuver often enough and with focus enough that it becomes rote, requiring a minimum of contemplation or planning,. And if such mental programing sounds a bit like "1984" for some of us that may not be an unreasonable price to pay.

Incidentally, do not keep readjusting your swing to fit each club selection or the peculiarities of an objectionable lie. Although she apparently never played the game, Gertrude Stein was absolutely right when she said that "a swing is a swing is a swing"—or something very much to that effect. While I was glancing through Nick Faldo's golf book, A Swing For Life, I was puzzled by the seeming duplication of photographs. I realized later, however, that although each photo was analyzing a different situation and was highlighting the use of a different club, the swinging motions were all almost identical. The variations were limited to the width of the stance and the fullness of the backswing, differing according to the length of the club and the distance of the target, but all of the other elements of the picture-perfect swing remained constant throughout: the same full pivot, the same smooth stretch, the same straight-armed follow-through—and the same flawless style for every club he used.

In summary, swinging a golf club should not be a particularly difficult or mysterious undertaking, but doing it in a way to satisfy the basic needs of a budding golf enthusiast requires more than just faith and instinct. It demands adherence to a set of rituals and routines and the adoption of some of the more obscure rules of physics in order to help guide man (and woman) through some of these difficult times:

- When lining up to address the ball, keep your mind and body relaxed and concentrate on just the matter at hand.

- Keep your body steady and your head immobile—before and all the way through the swing.

- Start the backswing as a single uniform motion, moving the hips, arms, shoulders, and club all together in absolute harmony.

- On your takeaway, pivot around an imaginary rod running through your head and torso, meanwhile stretching your arms and club to their maximum extension while taking special care not to shift the balance of your body. In order to achieve maximum coil, complete your backswing with your back facing the target, at which point your chin should be pressing down into your left shoulder.

- In order to help reduce the variables of the swing, keep the left arm firm and extended during the backswing, the downswing, and the early part of the follow-through. Remember, too, to keep the right elbow tucked into the hip during the beginning of the takeaway, then pointing downward when forced away from the hip by the body's turn.

- Although the speed of the swing may vary for each player, a more moderate and manageable pace during both the takeaway and the return to the ball encourages an escalation of speed at that instant of contact with the ball, which in turn is the most beneficial moment for increasing your power.

- Employ as much backswing and follow-through as you reasonably can, but do not try to push yourself beyond your capabilities. Tension is perhaps the most damaging ingredient of a good swing, so keep all the motions of the swing within the parameters of your own comfort zone.

8

THE LONG GAME

Nothing like the convenience of a good cliché to stop an analytic thought in its track. "Hit for show—putt for dough" is a case in point. Nice sound to it, but like most clichés it is so overworked that it can no longer impress those for whom the phrase was intended. Nevertheless, the fact remains that the long game counts for the least of your strokes. In my pre-Tom Simon days I could be banging away with my woods and long irons either well or badly and it made little difference to my total score. On a typical par-four hole, as an example, I could be within a wedge shot of the green in two if my drive and fairway shots went well, or within a 5-iron distance if not, or at least within easy chipping distance of the green in three even if all my long shots were terrible. But if it took an additional four or five strokes to find the hole, the difference of one lost stroke because of the quality of my long game wouldn't have had that much effect on my dismal total score.

On the other hand, all of that analysis is based on clearheaded logic, which often has very little to do with reality. The long game may have limited relevance to your total score, but it can be one of the more stimulating and gratifying facets of your total golf experience—a boon to your ego, your confidence and your reputation. Unfortunately, such a joyous accomplishment is not always within reach. On a busy day on the course, for example, when three or more foursomes are lined up awaiting their turns to tee off and the world's attention seems focused on your every move, a really bad drive (a highly likely consequence of self-doubt when subjected to all that pressure) can be devastating to one's self-respect. On the other hand, the confidence that derives from a well-hit drive can pay some serious dividends on the subsequent series of shots. The point is that in the vast scheme of things a good drive may not be all that important, but it surely can help keep the clouds away on a sunny afternoon.

The designation "long game" actually encompasses two different efforts. The first belongs to those shots using woods and long irons to significantly reduce the distance between you and the hole. The second is the next level up—hitting the ball farther than you are able, achieved by muscles you no longer have or by skills you have not yet acquired, but which defines your dreams and aspirations and is reached just often enough to keep those dreams alive.

In order to have any hope of reaching the second goal, the really long game, you must master all the basic components of a good golf swing, drilling them into your mind and your muscles until they are automatically reflected in your handling of almost any club you choose. In other words, it requires no magic—simply consistency. After you routinely manage your pivot and downswing and follow-through properly and the actions of your various limbs are invariably in sync, then you can safely and comfortably experiment with some of the variables of speed and timing and power that are the requisites of the really long game. Trying too hard to power the ball down the fairway while still struggling to implement the basics of the swing will more likely lead to digging deeper divots than to chasing longer balls.

Nevertheless, there are a few details worth noting that have special application for older golfers trying to make their long game longer. Several times throughout this book, for example, I refer to the necessity of slowing your swing and keeping your head down, but there is a tendency among seniors to ignore that advice when using woods or long irons. Probably because the thrill of crushing that ball a really long distance is so stimulating that the anticipation is too much to resist, so we lift our eyes and head to better view the results—which is an error of major proportions. Much better instead to concentrate on keeping your head perfectly still throughout the swing (as if caught between Tom's two-by-fours) and your fix eyes on the spot where the ball had been before contact.

Perhaps the most valuable maneuver for adding distance to your game begins with the backswing. About half way through the take-away, at about that moment in the swing when the shaft of the club is parallel to the ground, begin to cock your wrists so they are fully cocked by the time you reach the top of your backswing. The primary value of this is the vast amount of extra power you can bring to the swing by releasing those cocked wrists at just that moment of contact of the clubhead with the ball.

The mathematics of this phenomenon are better understood by considering the chapter on "The Swinging Game," which refers to the magnitude of the circumference of the circle traced by the path of the clubhead during its swing. By calculating the relationship between the short distance covered by hands traveling just a few inches (positioned as they are closer to the center of the circle of the swing) and the greatly expanded distance along the outside edge of that arc, you can see that unleashing the wrists at the appropriate moment will greatly increase the speed of the clubhead traveling along the swing's circumference.

Senior golfers sensitive about age-related athletic shortcomings might consider making one concession to the accumulating years: ratchet down the choice of clubs for driving and fairway wood shots. The longer shafts of the lower-numbered woods are meant to pound the ball ever further down the fairway, but that added distance, when you have not yet mastered all the many nuances of the swing, comes at a cost. I had found that the extra inch or two from grip to clubhead too often disrupted the rhythm of my swing and the consistency of my stroke, so until recently I restricted myself to using the shorter three-wood for driving and the five-or seven-wood on the fairway. Now, with confidence and competence restored by practice on the range and play on the course, I tee off with the driver and use the three-wood on the fairway, and with generally gratifying results. For a very long time, however, the more conservative approach provided me with straighter shots and adequate, albeit reduced, distances—a temporary concession to reality that was well worth that small loss of distance. Incidentally, that reliance on the shorter club off the tee is not applicable only to older hackers, but is a tactic often employed by many good players for at least the first few holes of a round, until they feel more secure in the rhythm of their swing.

In deference to what Tom sees as the reduced speed of both the minds and bodies of aging golfers, he has a bit of advice that should slow our swing while significantly improving our control. In the last chapter a recommendation was made to exert an extra twist of the body or a further extension of the club during the transition from the end of the backswing to the start of the downswing, the purpose of which was to trigger the turn of our hip and to help firm up our left side. Complementing that advice and covering much the same territory, but with an added benefit of improving contact between the clubhead and the ball, he has a further suggestion: at the start of the downswing let the grip-end of the club drop straight down for just a couple of inches before allowing the full downswing routine to take over. Don't force it, he says, but allow it to drop of its own accord, simply pulled by gravity. Beyond its value in setting the proper tempo and rhythm of the swing, this variation helps flatten the arc of the swing, greatly increasing the probability of the full face of the clubhead connecting squarely with the ball.

Also remember to keep the left elbow straight and locked during the entire backswing, the downswing and through the initial part of the follow-through. A common failing, even among the young and strong, is the tendency to search for still greater power in the swing, which somehow leads to bending the left elbow immediately after making contact with the ball. It does sometimes work, but resisting that temptation greatly improves the odds of adding both distance and directional control to the shot.

A hint that may come in handy for long fairway shots has to do with lining up the ball properly. Before settling into your stance, stand behind the ball and look toward your target area. Pick out an errant blade of grass or a weed or a piece of dirt somewhere in front of your ball in a direct line with the target and close enough to be seen while looking at the ball. Once you are lined up you need not look toward your target again—just swing your club along the path of that marker. This reassurance on direction helps free the mind to deal with other aspects of a swing that may not yet been fully automated. I also find this method valuable in trying to escape the confinement of a tree-blocked lie in the rough bordering the fairway. If I can see some reasonable window between a few of the trees, I use that marker method to improve my focus and my aim. I'm aided, too, by the observation of my friend, Dick, that trees are ninety percent air. That reassurance can be quite comforting—right up to the ball's collision with the remaining ten percent.

9

THE SHORT GAME

Even with all its ancillary problems, it is generally agreed that growing old is a lot better than the alternative. What is inadequately appreciated, however, is one of aging's little understood fringe benefits—the handy excuse it provides for a whole lot of poor performance. When our powerhouse drive peters out at 160 yards, for example, we can bury ourselves in the protective rationalization of our years ("Hey, c'mon now, for a guy my age?!") or compare ourselves to the mythical performance of times that never were ("Time was I coulda used a 5-iron for this shot.") On the other hand, for what is arguably the most decisive part of the game, where scores are built and diminished and where the money is won and lost, we have no acceptable excuse for screwing up. It doesn't take strength to make your mark around the green, after all, it only takes accuracy.

There are probably more shots lost on and near the green—silly little shots that have no right to go askew—than on any other part of the course, but these are shots that have nothing to do with strength or stamina. If we hit badly around the green and lose two or three strokes in the process, we can try to put the blame on Mame if we want, but implicating our age or arthritis or memory loss just won't fly.

For most golfers, about sixty percent of the strokes recorded on the score card are committed around the green, which doesn't leave the long game accountable for all that much of the total score. A bad drive, after all, can be overcome by a good second shot, and a bad fairway shot can be redeemed by substituting a wood or longer iron for what should have been the next short iron shot to the green, but a bad approach shot short of the green still leaves you short of the green. Or a badly aimed pitch may cover the distance, but still leave you no closer to the pin than before. Or a botched blast out of a sand trap can still leave you in the trap. The impact of badly executed shots while still out on the fairway, although troubling, can often be minimized by a good recovery, but errant short-game shots will cost strokes that cannot be overcome by whatever comes next…they are simply lost and irretrievable. The scorecard, after all, doesn't differentiate between long drives and short putts—a miss remains a miss and is just another stroke that must yet be counted.

And yet, despite the importance of mastering all the nuances of shots around the green, most amateur golfers spend their precious hours on the driving range struggling to improve their woods. If you have a choice between lowering your handicap through control of your short game and inflating your ego with great wood shots…I know, I know, most of us would choose the ego, but it really is a foolish decision.

FROM 50 TO 100+ YARDS OUT

The club selection for these distances depends solely on the strength and preference of the player, but beware of being misled by too seductive a memory. My performance while still in my fifties formulated my guideposts for selecting clubs, such as a 5-iron for 150 yards, an 8-iron for 135 yards, a pitching wedge for 100 yards, etc. I am now a couple of decades older and although that wrinkled face in the mirror is an unwelcome stranger, my power and vitality seem undiminished—I'm clearly as strong as I ever was. So it comes as rather a shock to discover that my 8-iron goes only about 125 yards and I need a 9-iron when I'm only 100 yards out. I tend to be a bit slow to learn, but it has finally dawned on me that all my short irons fall short and this can no longer be blamed on a strong headwind or a mismeasured marker.

When considering short iron shots, choose the right club to fly the distance if the ball is hit properly and with a full swing. In other words, keep your form consistent...don't adjust your swing according to the distance or club selection. The point is not to hit softly with a 9-iron, for example, if a full-stroke with a pitching wedge will do the job. On the other hand, of course, don't overswing an 8-iron to achieve a 7-iron's distance just because your younger opponent covered the distance with his 9-iron. In short, unnecessarily deviating from your customary swing, either by holding back or exerting more effort in order to accomplish a special purpose endangers the rhythm and character of the shot and should be avoided if possible. In order to reduce all superfluous thinking, keep your actions as rote as possible. The great American poet, Ralph Waldo Emerson, may have belittled such fidelity to form as a "foolish consistency, the hobgoblin of little minds," but then, Emerson never played golf. We should develop a swing that can be applied equally to all clubs in almost all circumstances—modified only in the degree of power that is brought to bear each time. It is that consistency, after all, that helps groove the swing and makes each shot more predictable and more accurate. A 9-iron swung easily and rhythmically, for example, is much more likely to yield the desired results than a pitching wedge wielded with the increased power necessary to achieve an extra five yards.

HEY, WHATEVER WORKS

Very simply, use the club that does the job, even if it is a lower numbered iron than the one your opponent has chosen...your fragile ego notwithstanding. This point is supported rather dramatically by one of Tom's experiences from several years ago. He was in a skins game (as defined in Chapter 16, "Variations Of The Game") consisting of three foursomes. The other players were sales representatives of several golf club manufacturers from around the country. Tom was about 65 at the time, whereas the others were all 30-year old hotshots who were primed to make a killing. At one point, with 12 competitors in the game, the carry-over skins on the upcoming 160-yard par-three hole were significant. One member of Tom's foursome used a mighty, well-controlled swing of his 8-iron off the tee and landed his ball within two feet of the hole, then busied himself planning the subsequent investments from his winnings. Tom, no longer as strong as in his earlier days, but just as confident, decided on the 6-iron as his weapon of choice—and holed out.

He knew the shot must have had a pretty powerful impact on the other players when a golf pro on the East Coast, one of Tom's former students, called to tell him that a sales rep was bitterly complaining of "some white-haired old fart who stole a s—-house full of skins" from him by hitting a hole-in-one. His friend didn't get a name, but from the description he knew it had to be Tom. Sure, the game has its frustrations, but how often in life are you blessed with similarly satisfying experiences?

CLOSE TO THE GREEN

Shots close to the green require a delicacy and finesse that is mostly personal and fall into no well-defined categories. The club selection for shots from a position close to the green could well be anything from the 7-iron up, depending upon your personal preference.

At about 30-40 yards out, for example, my preference (when I'm hitting well) is my lob wedge with its 60° loft (compared to the 48° loft of my pitching wedge), but only because I now have a renewed confidence in that club. That confidence translates into a crisp, clean shot that tends to do what I want.

The key variable in the choice of clubs when close to the green is the trajectory you hope to achieve: the greater the loft, the larger the margin of error, so when conditions permit, keep the ball low to the ground for better control. The most common variables to determine the choice of approach clubs include the hazards in front of the green and the size and slope of the green. If, for example, a bunker looms in front of the green and the size or contours of the green allows little space for the ball to roll before being off the green and in trouble, then a high loft and a dead stop are the choice of the moment. Otherwise, by keeping the ball closer to the ground and allowing it to roll onto the green, flawed shots are likely to less disastrous than those intended to fly high but, when struck badly, too easily go seriously awry.

Carrying the low trajectory approach to its extreme, when the ball is lying on a well-groomed fringe a short distance (perhaps 5-10 feet) off the green, a putter is the safest and most accurate shot available. If you take into account the inhibition of the roll because of the fringe grass and hit proportionately harder, chances are that on average you will fare better with the putter than you would with a chip shot, although putting with an 8-iron can be a very effective compromise (of which, more later).

All of this assumes that you can translate the theory into action, that you can indeed chip the 8-iron or 9-iron to a point on the green to allow the ball to roll the proscribed distance to the cup, or pitch with the lob wedge in such a controlled manner that it will fly near the cup and stop. At any rate, hours of practice on the chipping green using the technical advice counseled by Tom should significantly increase your confidence and performance for those shots very near the green.

Before pursuing perfection for the pitch shot and the chip shot, however, it is probably useful to understand the difference between the purpose of each:

> The chip shot is employed very close to the green, utilizing just enough loft to clear the intervening fringe of grass, then followed by a smooth roll on the green to the pin. (In fact, the shorter-distance chips are often referred to as "chip-putts.") The delicacy in its execution makes it highly unlikely that even a serious mishit can cause any real harm.

> The pitch shot, on the other hand, is from a position near enough to aim for the pin, but too far out (upward of 30 yards, depending on the strength and style of the player) to effectively predict and

utilize the roll of the ball on the green...at least at our level of expertise.

Chipping is the next move up from putting, a shot with a reasonable aspiration of getting the ball close to the pin and possibly into the hole. The pitch, however, despite the hope of sinking the shot, is realistically designed just to get the ball onto the green and preferably not too far from the hole. Whereas a properly executed chip shot is lifted slightly above the grass bordering the green then continues its roll lightly toward the hole, the pitch shot requires a more full stroke, employing more of a backswing and a greater use of the wrists, with the goal of increasing the loft in order to limit the subsequent forward role of the ball.

THE PITCH SHOT

The techniques for both pitching and chipping are very nearly the same, but there are a few significant differences. For example, whereas the chip shot demands that the body remain generally immobilized, allowing just the arms and shoulders to move (but only as a single entity), the pitch requires that you adopt a swing with a bit more rotation of the body, similar to that used for the mid-length clubs, although much more limited. The pitch is by definition a golf shot emphasizing loft, so a good stroke requires a timely hinging and releasing of the wrists on the way to and through the ball.

On the return of the clubhead to the ball during the downswing of a pitch shot, break the wrists somewhat so that the hands are ahead of the clubhead by the time it makes contact with the ball.

For those shots requiring a bare minimum roll after hitting the green, such as high shots over an intervening bunker or onto a green that rolls sharply to the back on the far side of the pin, seek maximum loft with a loft wedge or a sand wedge, striking sharply down on the back side of the ball in order to apply a small degree of backspin. To further decrease the amount of roll, rotate your right hand further than normal to the right, rolling it under the shaft. This reduces the forward spin on the ball so that when it hits the green it stops shorter than otherwise.

But the power and loft and other variables necessary to most effectively achieve our ends when fairly close to the green are matters not easily or uniformly resolved in the abstract. Gauging the power of the swing in order to achieve just the right distance for a pitch shot is one of the more valuable skills we can acquire, but also one that eludes most scientific methods of measurement. The distance the ball flies is totally dependent on the strength of the player, the length of the backswing, and the style of the swinging motion, none of which is subject to simple absolutes. Accordingly, we can only rely on the experiences of practice in order to determine how much swing best suits each of us. Simply and obviously, a short backswing will produce less distance, and a shorter one still less, but filling in the blanks on those measurements rests on each of our individual pairs of shoulders.

THE CHIP SHOT

To a large extent chipping, in technique and purpose and its quest for precision, is much like putting but from off the green. In a previous paragraph, for example, I made much of "trajectory" and the close relationship between loft and margin of error. This is a particularly important consideration for me when I'm badly off my short game. Instead of using my pitching wedge, for example, with which I might skull the shot and send it careening off to the other side of the green, I use an 8-

iron to lift the ball lightly over the intervening fringe grass, and roll it toward the cup. If I should happen to hit the ball badly, no real damage has been done except that I now have a longer putt (or two) to sink. That's a lot better than being off the other side of the green. Also, this fits with one of Tom's favorite aphorisms: "They don't ask you 'how'—they ask 'how many?'"

Unlike a fairway wood or a long iron shot in which a fairly small variation in distance or direction is of little consequence, the whole purpose of the chip shot centers on pin-point accuracy so that each little flaw in the grip or swinging motion can completely invalidate the effort and foolishly add strokes to the score. For such a shot, where the requisite level of precision is measured in fractions of an inch, it is important that all the body's moving parts remain as stable and quiet as possible during the swing.

At the start of the backswing for a chip shot, slide the clubhead straight back and low to the ground, avoiding the inclination to lift the clubhead up too soon in order to increase the power of the coming blow. Because the requisite distance to be covered is minimal, control is all-important, so keep the wrists firm.

On the takeaway, for example, keep the clubhead moving back in a low straight line and with your weight slightly favoring your left foot, stroking lightly through the ball with the back of the left hand and the palm of the right hand traveling toward the target. The need to keep your body's movements to a minimum can be aided by maintaining a light grip, choking down on the shaft of the club with the fingers just above the metal, and concentrating the power in the right hand. For added control rotate the left hand slightly to the left so that the thumb is just barely left of the center of the club grip, and keep the wrists rigid throughout. An effective method of keeping the wrists firm is to have the forefinger of the left hand overlap the middle two fingers of the right hand. This serves as a splint and makes improperly breaking the wrists a difficult and easily avoided action.

For a good chip shot, very much like putting, the key ingredient is stability. All excessive hand movements must be totally eliminated. The grip shown above is one way to help keep the hands and wrists steady and firm, thereby encouraging the clubhead to stay on a straight path to the ball.

This last bit of advice I offer hesitantly, because the experts are mixed in their assessment of whether the wrists should be firm or flexible for the slightly longer chip shots. Tom Watson recommends breaking the wrists on the takeaway, then keeping them in that position when coming back down and through the ball, a procedure that works well for me. Nick Faldo, on the other hand, believes "your swing [should] have flow...a quality that stems from the natural hinging and flexing of your wrist muscles." Faced with this array of conflicting recommendations, it is probably best to try them all and simply go with whatever it is that works best for you.

When lining up a chip shot, position the ball at the toe of the club rather than nearer the hosel (the junction of the clubhead with the shaft). The sweetspot on the clubhead face, that small place on the face nearer the toe, is larger than it is closer to the hosel, so aiming for that spot reduces the likelihood of shanking the ball. And once again, in order to maintain more solid control the distribution of weight should favor the left side during both the backswing and the follow-through, without any transfer of weight to the right.

Sweep the clubhead back in a low straight line, keeping the weight on the left foot, then follow through with the back of the left hand and the palm of the right hand traveling toward the target. The clubface should swing down under the ball when making contact.

A common and damaging tendency among amateurs (of any age) is to unconsciously alter the elevation of the clubhead—however slightly—from the start of the takeaway until its return to the ball. One fault may be that at the time of the setup we tend to stand with our knees slightly bent, placing a small additional percentage of the weight on the balls of our feet. When we complete the backswing and move the club forward to hit the ball we sometimes roll back on our heels, again only slightly, but enough to raise the elevation of the clubhead just a fraction. The result is that we may then strike the ball on its side rather than lofting it from below, thereby skulling the ball and propelling it across the green. The solution is to start the swing with the weight slightly on the heels, a procedure that greatly reduces that tendency to raise the elevation of the clubhead as it approaches the ball.

Meanwhile, as with all the other clubs in your bag, the pace of the swing remains of paramount importance…and personal. The speed and timing of the backswing and downswing should remain constant, keeping the left-hand grip very light while maintaining a slightly greater concentration of power in the right hand, and having the club-head accelerate through the ball. The arc and rhythm of the clubhead's movement to and through the ball is the same with these short clubs as it is with the woods and longer irons—flowing at a managed pace throughout the swing rather than sharply striking the ball, then quitting the forward motion after impact. Even for these very short approach shots the swing should be fluid rather than sporadic.

One of Tom's more novel ideas—and one that works surprisingly well—is using a fairway wood for chipping if the greenside fringe is significantly deeper than customary. He insists that because of the large flat sole of the clubhead there is less chance of "chilly-dipping," which sounds something like a cross between a barbecue and a clothes-free jump into the lake, but is a legitimate term referring to the club's chomping into the deep grass. I've tried it and it does seem to work, but I suspect its chief value for players like myself and my regular play-

ing partners may be more in disorienting the opposition than in changing the flight of the ball.

THE SAND TRAP—or—"The only thing to fear is fear itself." (FDR).

Along with most professionals, Tom insists that hitting out of the
sand is the easiest shot in the book. Perhaps so, but on the basis of the
experiences of my friends and myself that book must have been written
in Sanskrit. My friend Jarvis plays so much better than I that he usually
gives me five strokes a side and still walks away with the money. My hope
throughout the game, however, is that he lands in the trap—in which
case the hole is mine. One of the last times we played he hit the bunker of
a par-four hole on his second shot—and took an eight. He's not always
that successful; he's also been known to just pick up the ball and walk
away (mumbling). Of course, this could be overcome in time and with
lessons (which I have strenuously and thus far successfully discouraged),
but the trap so paralyses him that by now nothing less than hypnosis can
save him.

Well, that's not altogether true. He has pretty well perfected the
technique of putting out of traps, but only out of those that lack the
impediment of a large intervening lip (that overhang separating the
trap from the green). I've tried this myself but with less than limited
success, generally taking my next shot either from the same trap or its
sister off the other side of the green.

The fact is that for most of us the bunker is the ultimate challenge—to both our game and our increasingly fragile self-confidence.
That need not be the case and is an attitude derided by most professionals, but until we understand the basic rules of escape it will probably remain one of the primary causes of the amateur's nightmares.
This, incidentally, is a shot unaffected by youth and strength, which
means that there is no special "senior status" advice to give you an
edge. It also means that you have no legitimate excuse for failure.
Despite the vision of "blasting" out of traps, this shot generally requires

more rhythm than force. There are a number of different methods for hitting out of traps, depending on the distance from the green, the texture of the sand, the height of the rim between the trap and the green—and, of course, the personal preferences of the players. There are, however, certain general procedures that should be observed.

Address the ball with an open stance, using a swing that is loose, unhurried, and with a full follow-through. And take it easy! After all, using the heavy face of a sand wedge to make that little ball fly such a short distance does not take all that much force. Placement of the ball doesn't make much difference, but where the club hits the sand in relation to the ball does. The heavy flange on a sand wedge is designed to keep the club from burying itself in the sand, so it is best to hit about two to four inches behind the ball and with the clubface wide open, generating what is called a "splash shot." Properly executed, the ball is never actually touched by the clubface, but is lofted on a cushion of sand. It doesn't take much power to make the shot work, but it does take practice and the confidence that comes from having performed the shot well during that practice. Shuffle your feet into the sand in order to gain as much stability as possible, then swing loosely and softly, generating most of the power through your right hand, then conclude with a generous follow-through. The angle of the arc and the openness of clubface that you choose depend on a number of variables, such as the condition of the sand (wet, dry, packed, loose), the location of the ball with regard to the lip of the trap, and the distance of the pin from your location in the trap, but the most valuable advice is to practice—a lot—under varying conditions to develop your own sense of what works and what does not. For most amateurs caught in the trap, it is the fear that is their undoing, the fear of hitting too hard and landing far beyond the green, or the uncertainty of hitting too softly to escape the sand. That fear tends to inhibit the smooth flow of our swing—perhaps encouraging us to bend our left elbow on the follow-through, or to dig too deeply into the sand at impact—bypassing the basics that we know so well, justifying our fears and perpetuating the problem. Again, keep it smooth, keep it firm…and relax!

Address the ball with a slightly open stance, shuffle your feet into the sand for greater stability and swing loosely, hitting through the sand at about 2—4 inches behind the ball. Hitting out of a sand trap requires very little power—simply a smooth and fluid motion.

This chapter began with recognition of the importance of a good short game because it accounts for so much of our total score. The mere fact of our age can offer us no excuses for accumulating excessive short-game stokes, but a lot of practice and the increased confidence generated by ample and successful repetition can significantly improve our short game and have a very gratifying impact on our score. All that it requires is understanding and absorbing Tom's various short-game suggestions, then practicing them diligently. To help the process, I repeat the essence of his recommendations:

- For the longer approach shots try to avoid the temptation of showing off with a shorter club than you would otherwise be inclined to choose. For example, don't use an 8-iron to do the work of a 7-iron just because your partner covered the same distance with his 9-iron. On the other hand, if you are faced with an in-between distance, use the full swing of the shorter iron rather than adjusting the longer iron to a half-swing.

- For short pitches and chip shots to the green, the lower the trajectory the less chance of incurring damage from a shot hit badly, so use the less-lofted club whenever conditions permit.

- In starting the backswing for chip shots, sweep the clubhead back in a low straight line, keeping your weight on the left foot throughout, then follow through with the back of the left hand and right palm traveling toward the target.

- Grasp the club with hands lower on the shaft than usual, perhaps even to the point of touching the metal, and stand balanced on your heels rather than your toes.

The pitch is similar to the chip shot, with the exception of using a fuller swing and more wrist action.

For bunker (sand trap) shots using the sand wedge:

- The clubface should not touch the ball—keep a cushion of sand between the two.

- Use a very open clubface in the bunker, varying only somewhat according to the distance the ball has to travel and the condition of the sand.

- Shuffle your feet into the sand, keeping an open stance when addressing the ball to insure better stability, then accelerate the club beneath the ball—and follow through! Remember, it's not speed, it's not power…it's firmness.

10

THE PUTTING GAME

Some ancient theological theories are built on the belief that man was born cursed. The root cause of that curse, however, is in dispute, some tracing it to Adam feasting on Eve's apple at the urging of the wicked and manipulative snake. Others fault the earliest Greek gods and the curiosity of Pandora that unleashed on the world all the evils that were nestling in her mysterious box. Golfers may not agree on the genesis of the Curse, but they find no mystery in the nature of the Curse—it is clearly *the yips!*

Every once in a while and for no apparent reason, the putter seems to become an accursed instrument of the devil, obeying the irrational machinations of rebellious hands and of arms no longer controlled by the reasoned dictates of a rational brain. The hands that grip the club seem as strangers to the body that joins them, spasmodically jerking in short bursts of independent energy that might propel the ball three feet beyond a hole only two feet away. That is the condition known, feared and reviled as *the yips.*

Prayer and exorcism seem to offer some temporary relief, but the laity tend to prefer a more activist role, such as:

> (1) heaving the putter with all the strength you can muster in any direction you choose. With luck it might reach the lake and sink to its bottom or slam into a tree and break—in either case keeping the offensive weapon out of your view and releasing a lot of your inner tensions. Or…

(2) assigning the blame for the errant putt on the rotation of the earth or on the infestation of a rare and unique virus or, for those more inclined toward mysticism, on the likelihood that a dybbuk has invaded your body and that this is not really you, but some evil fifteenth-century monk (no one will believe you, but the exercise is designed to fool yourself, not your competitors). Or...

(3) insisting that the ball, wherever it might actually lie, is "within the leather," that distance between the grip and the bottom of the club and which, depending on a prior agreement, may constitute a "gimme." This may generate some rather heated disputes, but stand by your guns—losing a few friends is a small price to pay in such a crisis. Or...

(4) simply beat a hasty retreat to the 19th hole, choose a lonely spot in the corner, and search for the solution at the bottom of a glass.

If the measures listed above fail to offer satisfactory relief, don't collapse in self-pity and give up the game altogether. At least consider some of the other, more scientific alternatives that are available—and then you can resort to drink.

First of all, realize that alone among all the clubs in the bag there are almost no firm rules on how to hold or swing a putter. Putting remains a completely personal effort, so whatever inspires the most confidence and most effectively reduces the tension of the moment is the recommended procedure to adopt.

My friend Dick (the same guy whose saga of losing his club in the trees was recounted in Chapter 4, "The Mind Game") plays an excellent game between the tee and the green, but his uncertainty with the putter so unnerves him that he experiments with a different stance or swing almost every time we play. His latest effort for the short putt (up to about four feet) is to hold the club with just the left hand. Whether logical or psychological, it works for him and his newfound skill has temporarily ended the need for further experimentation. We're both pretty confident, however, that it won't last.

Many people (including Dick for the longer putts) have switched to a reverse grip (the left hand further down the shaft than the right) in order to attain the required stability and restore calm to his shaky hands and troubled soul. He tried this on Tom's recommendation, based on the theory that any change helps your concentration and that because the putting style is so personalized anyway that the switch is not about to break any sacred rules of golf. Whatever the logic, it does the job for him often enough that his feeling of comfort and relaxation when standing over the ball has been restored (for however long that may last) and is at least worthy of consideration by others equally desperate.

Without question, however, and far exceeding all the technical considerations, the most important factor in putting is the confidence the player has in stroking the ball. I have seen tall golfers almost doubled over to grasp very low on the shaft of a short putter, and players stand with both feet pointing parallel to the intended roll of the ball, and others with their feet in various spreads from almost touching to splayed out like they were trying to maintain balance in the face of a gale—all contortions which are designed to provide confidence and stability.

Incidentally, for whatever comfort you may derive from it, the yips are hardly the exclusive scourge of the amateur. Sam Snead, one of golf's premier players and a three-time winner of both the Master's and PGA tournaments, suffered miserably from it for so long that he seriously considered giving up the game altogether. On three consecutive holes in one tournament, for example, he missed putts of 12 inches, 18 inches, and again 12 inches. He remembered that he "felt like a zombie—like someone else's hands held the putter. All control had gone." In another tournament, when he was putting from 18 inches out, he jabbed the ball two feet past the hole, then jerked again coming back—for a three-putt.

He finally did overcome the yips, of course, mainly by adjusting to the science of putting. He immobilized his wrists during the stroke, extended the follow-through after striking the ball, and took more time to be comfortable in his putting stance. But most effective were the mind games he played. Instead of just assuming that the next shot would go awry, he learned to approach each shot with the confidence that he was in control. He changed his stroke and his putter and his outlook, and which of those adjustments was the most substantive is debatable, but it was enough to end his slump and enable him to become the all-time leader in PGA victories with a total of 81 wins to his credit. And that's the point: It makes no difference what ploy is used, whatever stance and grip and mindset inspires the most confidence will produce the best results.

Nevertheless, until you are discouraged by the results, there are some general truths about putting styles and habits that may be good starting points, all of which are easily revised or dropped if they don't work. Successful putting is largely dependent on three basic components: grip, swing, and stance, none of which, of course, is sacrosanct. You may substitute your own grip or swing or stance—as long as it is consistent and as long as it works. Tom's recommendations and my revisions and interpretations of those recommendations are not necessarily gospel, but they have greatly improved my own putting and may be of some help to others.

THE GRIP

Whatever the excuses, losing control of the putter (the yips) is clearly a psychological malfunction. Perhaps it is the anxiety of putting so much pressure on the importance of this one silly little maneuver, or maybe it is the realization that it has all come down to this one moment, this one stroke and the troubling uncertainty of being up to the challenge.

Whatever the cause, the resignation of the will in determining how and when the hands and arms move seems to encourage their independence and further robs you of control of the speed and direction of the swing of the putter.

The necessity, then, short of trading in your golf pro for a psychiatrist, is to deactivate the hands, a simple enough goal on paper but one that often seems unattainable when on the course. The essence of the correction is to somehow blend the arms, wrists and hands into a single entity, thus inhibiting the individual members from acting on their own. And all of that comes down to the grip, of which there are more varieties than there are golfers to apply them.

All the many methods of securing an easy and consistent flow of the putter include keeping the grip loose, the wrists firm and the arms straight, but within those parameters lie dozens of variations from which the afflicted golfer must choose. One is to extend the forefinger of the left hand over the two middle fingers of the right hand, forming a splint that makes it more difficult for the wrists to move on their own. Another splint design is to bend the left wrist backward in a sharp angle, thereby immobilizing it, then relaxing the muscles of the right hand as much as is reasonable, giving all the responsibility for control of the club to the rigid left hand. Or perhaps grasping the club along the life lines of the palms of the two hands, increasing the pressure of the thumbs on the shaft to keep the club firm. Another method, used by many professionals as well as old amateurs, is the reverse grip that I so dismissively attributed to Dick in one of the preceding paragraphs. By keeping the left hand lower on the shaft than the right and with its wrist cocked into a locked position, you assign control of the putter to the left hand, thereby reducing excess motion during the stroke and imparting a reliability to the steady movement of the putter and the power and direction of the putt. A similar procedure is to keep the right hand lower on the shaft in the more traditional manner, but with the right hand rotated far around to the right, thus eliminating the likelihood of flexing that wrist during the swing.

And the list goes on. In my own quest for mindless solutions to mind-numbing problems I've tried each of the above—several of them multiple times during the course of just a single round—and have finally decided that it's all in my head, so I have gone back to the source of the problem, applying logic and dealing with the problem intellectually. The first essential is to relax! If you feel a bit unsure of yourself when standing up to the ball—even if it is only two feet from the hole—walk away and begin again.

Because two of the essentials for a good putting performance are confidence and inflexibility, reassess your grip and stroke and go back to the basics. By keeping your grip light and wrists firm, you can concentrate instead on the speed and direction of the stroke. Arguably the most valuable recommendation you might consider is to freeze your shoulders, arms and hands into a triangle, moving them all together like a pendulum, swinging smoothly, uniformly, and without jerky variations. The pendulum position helps inhibit all extraneous movements,

Unfortunately, too often all of this calm, objective analysis means diddly-squat when you're hunched over the putter, just short of the hole and with a double-press staring you in the face. Golfers paralyzed in anticipation of the upcoming three-foot putt and trying to outwit the demons of the damned who beckon from beyond the hole may need something more reliable than pure thoughts, so all those alternative grips and procedures should be kept on hold. But for my money, if the fault is in the mind, then I'm inclined to seek the solution in the mind…at least until something better comes along.

THE STROKE

When using a wood or long iron, hitting the ball a couple of hundred yards with fairly good direction is the goal. If you're off the mark by a few feet, so what? On the green, however, being off-line by half an inch adds an extra stroke to your score—maybe two if you miss the putt coming back. Unwavering concentration, then, is necessary to keep the ball on a direct path to the hole without any damaging side-trips, so it is important to keep the putter head traveling in a straight line. I realize this observation is about as profound as discovering that the best way to hit a home run is to hit the ball out of the park, but deviation in the path of the putter's clubhead is a very common and damaging flaw, so make certain that throughout the swing—in both its takeaway and its follow-through—the club adheres to the unwavering line that leads straight to its target.

Most professional golf instructors insist that the distance the putter head travels before and after making contact with the ball should be identical. Most instructors say it, so it must be right...but that does not necessarily make it right for everyone. I have determined that extending my follow-through by a couple of inches more than my takeaway (such as moving the putter head about eight inches beyond the ball after having first gone back about six inches) offers better control of the speed and direction of the ball. By sliding the clubhead straight back very close to the ground, I find that the longer follow-through enables me to keep the head of the putter moving in a straight line toward the hole—and, for me at least, has proven to be a very successful and satisfying procedure.

Incidentally, that inviolable maxim of always keeping your eye on the ball, like all other inviolable maxims, is open to occasional debate. Paul, a fellow member of our "Thursday Night Poker and Occasional Golf Club" (who appears again in the next chapter on "Course Management") recently gave me a very valuable putting tip which turns that eternal truth on its head and with very satisfying results. He suggests keeping the eye on the head of the putter throughout the stroke as another calming defense against the yips. By first determining the proper path for the ball to reach the hole, then gauging the requisite power to roll the distance, you can concentrate more fully on the details of the strike itself—such as keeping the clubhead true to the line of flight and meeting the ball on the dead center of the clubface—than on all the incidentals of getting there. And it works! I'm not sure why it works, maybe it's a delusion (Descartes might say, "I think it works, therefore it works") but whatever the reason, it has saved me a barrel of strokes and a lot of embarrassment.

THE SPOT PUTT

Faithfully following through on the perceived line of roll when executing a long putt can sometimes be a difficult and disconcerting task. Part of the problem is the different relationship that exists between the eye and the ball when peering down from above as opposed to looking at the ball from behind. That changed vantage point provides a different view of the ball's path to the cup. One way to overcome the problem, at least for longer putts, is the spot putt, a procedure similar to the one mentioned in Chapter 8, "The Long Game," for use with the fairway woods. Pick out a spot on the green (a distinctive blade of grass or piece of sand) somewhere along the chosen path to the target, then aim for that spot. This routine is not necessary for most putts, but it does help with those that are a significant distance from the pin.

My friend Peter uses a slightly different variation of the "spot putt" with great success. His game is only adequate, but his deadly performance on the green is quite enough to make him a serious contender. His secret, besides his impenetrable concentration, is the way in which he lines up the ball. By repositioning it on the green with a line of printed copy (usually the manufacturer's name) pointing toward the target, he can concentrate more on the requisite distance than on the direction. This procedure, I have since discovered, is a common practice among many of the game's professionals as well.

THE STANCE

Where and how you stand to begin the swing can also play an important role in how you strike the ball and in the confidence you bring to the task. Arnie Palmer, for example, winner of 92 of the world' most prestigious golfing awards since the early 1950s, stands so knockneed that his knees actually touch, giving his lower torso the appearance of an ambulatory X. A less offbeat procedure is to position the ball slightly to your left at set-up, with your weight favoring your left side. This helps to achieve the extended follow-through mentioned above, and by bringing the clubhead back straight and low to the ground is more likely to help the ball in keeping to the target line toward the hole. Further, positioning the ball slightly to the left of your gravitational center imparts a little overspin to the ball, allowing a more gentle stroke propel it toward the hole.

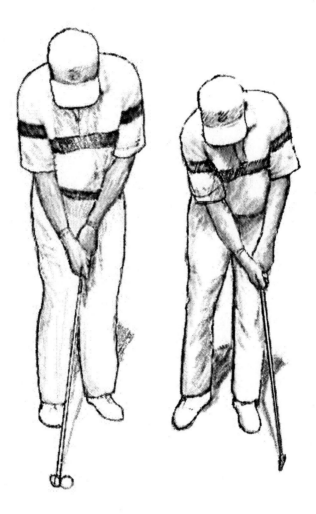

With your head tilted slightly to the right, it is less likely to move with the action of your arms. Keep the putter no more than an inflexible extension of your arms, limiting all movement to the shoulders. Body weight should favor the left side, then follow-through with the club-head continuing in a staright line to the hole.

One of the more common faults in golf, common to all shots from the drive to the chip to the putt, is lifting the eyes when making contact with the ball in order to see what is happening. Unintentional, of course, but a big mistake. By so doing you tend to move your head and alter the performance of the swing, too often changing the flight path of the ball or the elevation of the clubhead when making contact with the ball, inviting a divot on the fairway or a skulled shot near the green—or a slightly misdirected shot on the green…which is less dramatic than the other mishits, but just as costly. When putting, as with just about every other shot in your bag, keep your head down, your weight somewhat on your heels and your clubhead flowing.

To recap, the single most important factor in putting well is confidence—the confidence that you know the line, that you have the right speed, and that the ball will indeed go where you intend. Stepping up to the ball for a crucial putt and facing that task without fear or doubt has got to have a positive impact on the way you stroke the ball.

David Duval can attest to that. Duval, ranked third among the world's top professional golfers, asserts that confidence is "96 to 97 percent of putting" and spends more time practicing his chipping and putting than his driving. "My short game saved me my first year," he recalled in an interview with The New York Times. "I left the West Coast my rookie year third on the money list. I had learned then what it could do, how much it could help you, how much it would pay off." That confidence, he says, is a hard-won benefit, gained from endless hours of hard work on and near the practice green. "It comes from facing different situations and making putts. It comes from knowing you've worked on the right things, so when you get under the gun, you can execute what you've practiced." "You can be a good putter," he insists, "and make a lot of putts, but can you do it when you need to do it on Sunday to win a tournament? There's a difference."

Or, as Davis Love, winner of 13 PGA tour titles, reminds us, "One putt a round can take you from 150th on the money list to the top ten." How's that for encouraging a relaxed attitude when you're trying to line up your next putt?

11

COURSE MANAGEMENT

Perhaps because I live in a university town (Ann Arbor, home of the University of Michigan), my introduction to the phrase "course management" left me searching for the clarifying identification of "101." It does not, however, refer to a business school course or some other element of academia, but simply to an analysis of some of the demons bedeviling many of the game's unsuspecting amateurs. Course management is really little more than an exercise in self-discipline and logic, a system whereby one can avoid some of the more foolish and unnecessary errors of judgment that tend to plague poor and moderate golfers and to prevent those beleaguered victims from making still more foolish and costly mistakes through faulty judgment.

Golf, after all, is the sport of optimists—why else would so many of us still be with it after so many decades of hacking away with so little to show for it? So it should come as no surprise that many of us tend to assume that we'll miss that overhanging branch or clear the water hazard or lift the ball lightly out of those deep, dense weeds of the rough. If early in my search for golf proficiency I had been wise enough and clearheaded enough to consider and deal with the likelihood of such abject failure I might have traded in my golf clubs for a chess board and led a more bland and sedentary life, but like most people I tend to shape my life through fantasies. For the last fifty years I have been so convinced of my own inherent skills that I have refused to recognize my otherwise obvious athletic shortcomings. The result is an irrational confidence that blinds me to my own realities and prompts me now to waste an extra three strokes in an aborted effort to save just one.

Course management refers to playing the game with a modicum of logic, a reasonable sense of caution, and an understanding—and acceptance—of one's own athletic limitations. It suggests balancing the downside of a failed risk with the potential benefits of its limited likelihood of success, asking that you exhibit enough self-discipline not to be victimized by an irrational optimism. That self-discipline may come into play, for example, when you curb your desire to use your 3-wood in order to pound your next shot over the lake and onto the green instead of playing short in order to set yourself up for an easy wedge shot to the pin.

A debacle played out a few years ago with my friends Sid and Saul on the 18th hole at Washtenaw Country Club effectively illustrates my point.

The 18th is not a particularly difficult hole, but chances are that after your drive you will still be left with about 160 to 170 yards to the green That should not be very daunting, but beginning at about 90 yards out is a lake that floats obliquely up to the green, then wraps itself half way around the right side of the green. Given the limited margin for error, the odds favor laying up just short of the water, but most players of any reasonable amount of either skill or ego will go for the green on their second shot. Both of my friends, mid-nineties players, amply fulfilled both preconditions, so they naturally went for broke. As sometimes happens, however, they both dropped short and into the water. Between us we had about a dozen different bets going (fortunately Saul was an accountant in real life), so their bodies tensed and their swings deteriorated as the pressures mounted. Saul hit his next shot into the water again, as did Sid, then again…and again…for a total of four shots into the lake for each of them—accompanied by an increasingly burdensome debt load. Eventually, their natural skills and belatedly relaxed muscles took over and they were able to clear the water and reach the green. (It was some years later that a similar tragedy was fictionalized and became the focus of the movie, Tin Cup.)

The problem was that because of the pressures of both the pride and the purse, they kept playing the long shot rather than the safe shot. Self-discipline, as it relates to good course management, means you choose the wise shot over the chancy shot. This may mean you put away the driver with which you have been having trouble and finish the game teeing off with a 3-wood or a 4-iron. Self-discipline may be hard to exercise, but it often reveals itself as the triumph of common sense over ego.

On the other hand, sometimes, for the sake of your ego you don't always want to be practical. In much the same irrational fashion that the touring pro in Tin Cup kept hitting ball after ball into the lake, you simply have to take the challenge and go for it. If you can keep it from becoming a habit, the exhilaration of even occasional success is more than worth the pain of more frequent failure.

Just don't expect me to bet on your team.

The other ingredient essential for good course management is making the proper club selection, an important factor too often triggered by bravado substituting for logic. It is also one that unfortunately tends to kick in a bit too late to be of much help, often accompanied by the reflection that "I shoulda used my x iron." Beside the eighteenth, for example, there are several holes on my home course on which the front edge of the green bumps up against a stream or a lake. When the pin placement is near the front, good course management suggests that we not aim for the pin, but rather play for the middle or even the far edge of the green in order to avoid a pointless penalty. An extra long putt, after all, is far less demoralizing—or costly—than fishing a ball out of the water.

Aside from choosing the right club to properly handle the distance, good club selection must take into account the occasional need to avoid other potential hazards. The spreading branches of an intervening tree, for example, may make it advisable to use a longer iron with limited loft rather than risk the satisfaction of a high lob that looks pretty but is endangered by wayward tree limbs.

Most strategies for good course management have nothing to do with the technical skills that generally elude us in our pursuit of lower scores, but are simply the obvious decisions of reasonable people at play. Of course, the root bases of good golf—the proper swing and grip and stance—are forever in the background for all of our efforts, but it is the reasons underlying each of our moves that may have a larger impact on our game. An example of this concern for the simple application of logic in golf is Tom's instruction to "play the shot that tends to favor your next shot." That may not be profound, but it is extremely valuable and becomes more meaningful and clear around the green.

For example, when still off the green or a long distance from the pin on a sloping green, you would be well advised to choose a spot below the hole as your primary target rather than aim for the pin and risk ending up above the hole. By leaving yourself with an uphill putt you will have a much easier and very much less dangerous second shot than with a downhill putt that could miss the hole and just keep on rolling.

A more obvious example of course management, one that particularly bedevils me as a curse of my unfortunately unwarranted optimism, is simply not to throw away one or more shots on improbable dreams When you have hit into the dense, but not quite impenetrable cluster of trees bordering the fairway and can find no clear shot in the general direction of the green, the sensible move is to take a safe lateral shot to the open fairway. Too many of us tend to be so tormented by the prospect of throwing away still another stroke and are so desperate to get at least some advantageous distance from my next shot, that we desperately embrace my friend Dick's theory that those big trees with the spreading branches are really 90 percent air, so I hit with high hopes (even if with low expectations), aiming for that little opening between the big oak and the pine, avoiding the branches of those cottonwoods, etc. The perfectly predictable, almost inevitable result, of course, is that I hit the tree in front of me so that my ball bounces off to the side and even deeper into the woods—altogether costing me three extra strokes instead of just one…and probably a new ball in the bargain.

A much wiser course of action is simply to take your medicine and play it smart. If your drive winds up in among the trees bordering the fairway, aim not necessarily for the green, but for the most unobstructed route out of the woods. If a reasonable path forward can be found, then of course take it, but only if the odds are clearly in your favor. If a less dangerous alternative is laterally onto the fairway, by all means go there. Wasting a shot to escape confinement in the wood is a small price to pay for freedom, a stroke easily made up when on or near the green. Hitting a tree while trying to make your escape, however, could well add several strokes and a whole lot of trauma to your game…and it's just not worth it. On the other hand, if you do decide to break out of your confinement but are hemmed in by tall bushy trees that work against lofted flight, consider using a 3-iron to hit the ball from farther back in the stance, somewhat off the right heel and keeping the clubhead low to the ground. The point is to sufficiently reduce the trajectory of the ball to keep it below the threats posed by the trees branches.

The conflicting approaches—hit laterally to get out of the woods, or toward the hole with a low shot to avoid the trees—highlights the main problem facing an aggressive and optimistic golfer. There is no hard and fast rule by which to determine your best escape from trouble—as with poker, it's all in the odds. Once again, if the foliage between your ball and your target is relatively sparse and the trees are spaced so that windows through them are not too narrow or harrowing, then perhaps you should take a chance and go for it. If, on the other hand, the intervening hazards leave you less than secure about the likelihood of reaching a clearing unscathed, then it is probably wiser to shoot for safety than for gain. Ultimately, however, although objective factors come into play, the issue is one of subjective judgment—and ego.

Another hazardous tilt at windmills lies in trying to effect a shortcut when presented with a fairway dogleg (a turn in the fairway that thwarts a straight shot toward the green). On a sharp dogleg around a cluster of trees, for example, don't try to cut it too closely. True, if you succeed you may save 30 or 40 yards on your next shot, but it's generally not worth the risk. It is much wiser in terms of course management to play it safe. Generally, on a par-four hole of average length with a significant dogleg, for example, it is questionable that you're going to hit the green in two anyway, so the smart choice is to concentrate on driving to some place on the fairway that will afford a clear line of sight to the green. In most cases the only real difference between the two shots is that your third shot to the green will be a mid-iron instead of a wedge. As senior amateurs with our level of strength and expertise, the benefit of the gamble hardly justifies the potential risk.

Unfortunately, I know whereof I speak. The second hole at Radrick Farms, one of the University of Michigan's two golf courses, has a sharp dogleg to the left, around a forbidding protrusion of tall trees and dense scrub. The ideal drive will tightly cut the woods, leaving the ball positioned forward on the fairway about 165 yards short of the highly elevated green. The alternative is to aim for the center of the fairway, which will leave you with somewhere between 200 yards to 230 yards and two strokes from the green. My inclination is to try to save one of those two strokes, so I carefully attempt to skim the edge of the woods on my drive. More often than not, of course, I miss my goal by just enough to wind up in the woods, behind a couple of massive old oak trees, invariably costing me at least one extra stroke—and perhaps another lost ball in the bargain.

Who am I kidding? Even if I hit the drive well, the likelihood of my reaching an elevated green 165 yards away on the next shot is very limited. If, on the other hand, I hit only a fair drive down the right side of the fairway with about 230 yards to the green, my next shot should put it within an easy wedge to the green. Over the years, that second hole has proven to be a very expensive piece of real estate for me

12

IN A NUTSHELL

And then there is the story about the 70-year-old man who went to a priest for confession.

"I have been very bad. Last week I met a lovely young lady at the movie theater. We had a drink together, then we went back to my place where we made love all evening long. The next day we made love again, once in the afternoon and twice more in the evening. Then on the following day before taking her to the train station for her trip home we made love still again."

"A young girl?" the priest asked.

"About twenty or twenty-one," the old man estimated, "and beautiful."

"Indeed," the priest noted, "you have been bad. But tell me—your accent puzzles me. What is your name?"

"Sam Ginsburg, your honor."

"Sam Ginsburg? But you're not Catholic. I can't give you absolution. Why are you telling me this?"

"Why? Because at my age, with a story like this, I'm telling everyone I can find."

After more than a half-century of playing grossly inadequate golf, what justification have I for giving technical advice and sounding like an accomplished winner? Well, like old Sam Ginsburg, I'm so pleased at having brought my scores down from 115 and above to the mid-nineties that I'm telling everyone who will listen just how I did it and how good it feels.

There is no single secret of success, of course. There is no special grip, for example, or radical new swing plane or exotic new stance that is going to provide the power and direction and control that had hitherto been missing from a golfer's repertoire. Nor is there some special mystical power we can call upon, like the mumble of some obscure ancient Hindu chant to invoke the divine influence of our personal golf god. The sad but inevitable reality is that competence in hitting the ball with some fair degree of power and control demands a solid understanding of all the many details of the golf swing followed by hours of repetition until the results become a naturally ingrained and automatic part of your game.

The problems are matters of patience and faith. After endless hours on the driving range and countless frustrating days on the golf course, all of which had combined to prove that your game was hopeless and that you could never reach the higher level of barely competent, there may well come a moment when it really does all come together. At least it did for me.

Having been shown the basics by Tom, remembering some only occasionally and grooving others into my memory bank by constant repetition, I found myself ready for the next step in the progression. I didn't really expect a dramatic breakthrough and was unprepared for it when it occurred, but one day it just happened. I was concentrating on all the myriad facets of the swing that had been poured into me by Tom (and at least somewhat reinforced by my endless hours of practice on the range) when it occurred to me that—yes!—I should add a touch more power with my right hand, and that I needed to pivot just a bit more completely on my takeaway, and that my downswing was still just a bit too fast. I adjusted my swing accordingly—and it was like adding a pebble to a fully saturated lake. The addition, however insignificant it may have seemed, was just enough to raise the level and make the entire system overflow. Suddenly, my drives went farther and straighter, my lofted irons flew higher and more sure, and for the first time I felt like I was in control.

And that was the real magic of that moment. It was my realization that all those hours on the practice range had a purpose, that each of Tom's large and little changes in the different elements of my swing fit a pattern—and that the pattern made sense. There remain, of course, more than a few rungs that I keep missing on my climb up the ladder of proficiency, but I have the immense satisfaction of knowing that I can do it, that however much I might continue to screw up I have within me the basic skills necessary to make me a competitor—not a major competitor, to be sure, but at least an adequate one.

Precisely what small corrections in the game will trigger such a moment for others is, of course, impossible to say, but that they exist and are hiding in the shadows of the mind is reasonable to assume. I simply wish to reassure other frustrated hackers that despite the anxiety of never being able to make the ball do what it was assigned to do, all that time and practice and embarrassment has not necessarily been wasted. Improvement is a generally slow and incremental process, but after adequate immersion in all the details of a good swing, a sudden break in the logjam remains a very real and encouraging possibility. It happened to me and regularly happens to others. What follows, then, is simply a nutshell version of some the discoveries I have found to be most valuable for my game:

1. Whether seeking distance with the driver or loft with the wedge, consistency in the style of the swing is paramount. Some of the variables will have to be modified, of course, to meet the specific needs of the pending shot, but the larger details and style of the swing itself remain essentially unchanged. In short, except for a few details in some limited instances, do not revise your swing to meet imagined needs of each separate club or situation.

2. The early part of the takeaway sets the pace for which most everything else follows, so the three component parts of that

action have a special responsibility. First, begin your movement with all parts of your body generally moving as a single entity, forgoing all independence of your arms or shoulders or torso. Secondly, sweep the clubhead straight back close to the ground, avoiding the tendency to lift it into its attack mode too soon. This flattens the arc of the swing, making it much more likely that the subsequent return of the clubhead to the ball will be square. Finally, keep the right elbow close to your body, perhaps even tucked into your waist until the fullness of the backswing forces it to move out, but then keep it pointed toward the ground rather than off to the side.

3. A properly performed pivot is absolutely essential both for maintaining a good balance (as opposed to allowing too great a shift to the right side during the takeaway) and for achieving the tight coil necessary for adding power to the stroke. The evidence of the full and completed pivot is that at its conclusion your back should be facing directly towards the target, leaving you prepared to unwind with the full power of which you are capable.

4. At the conclusion of the pivot there is a momentary pause marking the transition from the end of the backswing to the beginning the downswing. By using that pause as a stimulus for the turn of the hips preliminary to the rest of the body's participation in the downswing phase, my clubhead is more likely to meet the ball sharply at the end of the swing, enabling me to explode through the ball for greatly improved distance and control. Complementary to that procedure is the act of allowing the grip-end of the club to drop just a few inches at the start of the downswing. This helps flatten the arc of the clubhead during its approach to the ball, thereby improving the likelihood of striking the ball squarely and with greater force.

5. It is important to keep the left elbow straight during the take-away and downswing and through the early stages of the follow-through until other demands of the swing and limitations of the body supersede. This procedure helps keep the number of variables to a minimum, improving the consistency of the swing, and improves the odds of making good contact with the ball. The straight-elbowed follow-through helps insure that the path of the clubhead through the ball will be extended into the flight of the ball, increasing the probability of maintaining the direction of its continuing journey. Adding to the effectiveness of that procedure, I then try to finish the move with my arms high and the grip-end of the club pointing toward the target.

6. Gripping the club too tightly with either hand has a seriously damaging impact on both the control and the power of the swing, introducing a tension that inhibits the rhythm and smooth flow of the total process. Especially damaging to the shot, however, is the effect of a tightened left hand grip, which tends to make the wrist too rigid to straighten out sufficiently at the time of impact. A still-cocked wrist at that juncture is likely to result in the clubhead meeting the ball with an open face, sending it careening sharply off to the right Further, by losing the extra speed that a timely release of the cocked wrist would have generated, the clubhead fails to achieve the full potential of its power as it moves through the ball, unnecessarily limiting the distance and control that is otherwise available.

7. It has been mentioned a number of times earlier, but it is worth repeating: maintaining a constant and moderate speed during the downswing, then accelerating, or exploding, through the ball from about the moment of contact is one of the more effective ways of ways of increasing both the power and control of the strike.

8. After I have set up, but just prior to the takeaway, I twist my head slightly to the right (not extremely, but comfortably so), until I get the sensation of peering down on the ball slightly more with my left eye than with both. This helps stabilize my head and my swing and provides an additional and welcome degree of uniformity to the whole process.

9. When properly positioned in front of the ball at the setup and prepared to start my takeaway, I have learned to wait for a few seconds before launching into my swing. This pause enables me to focus my mind on some of the more important elements of the swing that I'm about to initiate and encourages a valuable relaxation of my body and my mind.

10. Recommendations for shots near the green vary widely, but I find the greatest success is too cock my wrists, then drag the clubhead straight back fairly and low to the ground. With the grip of both hands light and relaxed, albeit with a slightly greater concentration of power in my right hand, I then strike through the ball, extending the back of my left hand and the palm of my right hand toward the target. I concentrate my weight a bit more heavily on my left foot and limit my swing to just my arms and shoulders, employing no wrist action whatsoever. The longer approach shots require essentially the same procedures, except that I employ a bit more wrist action in order to gain more distance without changing any other element of the swing.

   One problem with the short chip shot is the tendency to roll back on your heels during the backswing, causing the clubhead to meet the ball at a slightly higher elevation than intended. I have overcome that by keeping my weight slightly on my heels at the time of setup, thereby maintaining a constant elevation before and through the shot.

11. Control of the putter is vastly increased by eliminating all independent flexibility of the arms, hands or wrists. Perhaps the most effective way to accomplish this is to have your shoulders, arms and wrists frozen together in the form of a triangle, then assume the dependable rhythmic motion of a pendulum.

I find, too, that the direction of my putt is better controlled by encouraging the putter head to flow toward the hole after meeting the ball, rather than stopping too soon after making contact. I do this by maintaining a follow-through along the targeted path for a distance slightly greater than that of the takeaway, meanwhile keeping my wrists firm, my head down and bringing the putter head back close to the ground.

There is, of course, nothing sacred about this list. Every golfer has his/her own list of must-do's and should-do's and better-not-do's in their search for perfection—or adequacy—but this is my nutshell and these are the tips that worked for me.

13

REFLECTIONS

During all those years of toiling in the salt mines and dreaming of retirement, most of us thought that simply settling back with a good book would be like a stroll through the gates of Paradise. Well, so much for plans built on fantasy—which leaves us golf.

The game is played for a variety of reasons, almost none of which has anything to do with the scorecard. A low handicap is fine, but more often than not it is a goal to reach rather than a condition to enjoy. However badly we play there is always the expectation, justified or not, of improvement—and that is the energizing, soul-satisfying value of the game. It's not how you play the game, but how you play the game today compared to yesterday, and although hitting well is good, for many of us simply hitting better is just as good.

One of the more appealing characteristics of golf is its application for otherwise ordinary people. We need not have the strength and grace of the young, golden-haired athlete to excel in the game—just determined will do quite well. I'm writing this not long after the death of Ben Hogan, one of the greatest of all the legendary figures of golf, so I am particularly sensitive to the role that strength of character has to play in the sport.

Ben Hogan, the winner of four United States Open Championships, two United States Masters tournaments, two United States PGA tournaments and one British Open, was clearly one of the premier golfers of all time, but by his own admission he was not naturally athletic. In fact, it was not until he was in his late twenties that it finally became clear that he might indeed make a living as a professional golfer. As for strength, he was permanently and painfully crippled by a near-fatal car accident in his thirties and continued to suffer, almost unable to walk, for the rest of his life. But it was not until some years after that disabling trauma, still in pain and seriously limited in his walk and his swing, that he achieved some of his greatest golfing victories. The point of this tribute is to repeat and lend substance to Tom's and my comments earlier in the book that the mind, in both its attitude and its concentration, plays the single most important role in the achievement of golfing skills. And that should give comfort to at least some of us sidelined wannabes who still fantasize about achievements presumably beyond our reach.

Another one of golf's Greats, a friend and mentor to Tom in his youth, was Byron Nelson, Hogan's boyhood friend and worthy competitor. When I was preparing to write this book, Tom gave me a copy of Nelson's Winning Golf, written in 1946, a relatively recent tome for readers and players my age, although perhaps considered an ancient manuscript by youngsters playing the game today. It was an interesting book in a number of ways, but especially as an example of how very much the game has changed from that day to this—and of how remarkably similar it has remained.

The status of the game of golf was a bit different at about mid-century than it is today. Nelson, for example, had been winning major international golf tournaments since 1937 and enjoying a level of success and fame familiar to only a handful of golfers throughout the history of the game. In 1945, he became (and remains today) the only golfer ever to win eleven consecutive major golf tournaments, and through this remarkable achievement he was able to boost his winnings to a total of $35,000...for the entire year!...a new world's record for earnings in professional golf. For the sake of comparison, I just finished watching Tom Lehman win $1 million for a single tournament! Times do indeed change.

Golf equipment in the forties was as different as were the rewards. In addition to the driver, the brassie (now the 2-wood), and the spoon (now the 3-or 4-wood), Nelson recommended carrying all the irons numbered one through eight plus the niblick (now the 9-iron) and as an afterthought added that it would be nice, too, if they could be a matched set. And there's probably nothing wrong with owning a golf glove, he observed, but noted that professionals rarely used them.

Despite the revolutionary changes in today's equipment, however, Nelson's instructions on the technical aspects of the swing are almost identical to those taught today, including the admonition that "the best golf is the easiest golf," advice still lauded and repeated by Tom Simon and other teachers of the game. The equipment may now be high-tech, and the design of the golf courses and the methods of teaching have improved immeasurably from then until now, but the mechanics of the game—the swing and the grip and the stance and all the other elements of the stroke—are essentially unchanged. Which should come as no surprise. After all, the basic laws of physics, recognized thousands of years ago by Archimedes, then later by Galileo and the other ancient intellectual giants, are constant and immutable. They remained as true for the building of the Empire State Building as they had been for the construction of the Egyptian Pyramids—or for determining the flight of a golf ball. Tom, too, understood the truth of this, as evidenced by his disdainful reply to my question about whether to replace my old irons with brand X or brand Y: "It makes no difference—you still have to hit the ball." In these days of overheated promotions and rapid-fire changes, of titanium or uranium shafts and four-metal super jumbo heads and perma-grip gloves or whatever, that small factor of cosmic stability—the fact that I still have to rely on my own swing—is somehow reassuring despite its depressing aspects.

Meanwhile, however obscure it may be, there is a special magic about the game of golf that grips most players and never lets go. It may elude those who don't play the game, but Arthur Daly, a sports columnist, recognized it when he wrote,

> "Golf is like a love affair. If you don't take it seriously, it's not
> any fun. If you do take it seriously, it will break your heart."

For some people, playing golf follows the familiar pattern of such addictions as alcohol or gambling but without the same damaging downside. For many years Rick, a sales representative I know from California, spent about eight months of each year on the road. His routine would be to time his client visits so that he would be near a golf course almost every day of his trip, and if unable to arrange a game with his customers, would build his work schedule around his morning or afternoon tee time. A personality dispute with his boss (having nothing to do with his golf or his sales performance) led to his resignation but not to a change in his routine. As an unemployed but still adequately affluent salesman, Rick continues to visit the same courses for much the same schedule for most of the year. His children are grown and out of the house, and I know that he is very fond of his wife—but he dearly loves his golf.

The enjoyment of golf derives from many factors, such as the simple social aspect of spending a pleasant afternoon outdoors with your friends, or the delight in winning money or acclaim from them, or simply the thrill of the competition. But stripped to its essentials, golf needs no adversary against whom to measure your talents, no "victory" to be fulfilling. It can be enough just to compete against yourself—against who you were yesterday and measured against who you would like to be tomorrow. It is true that without a witness a really good drive or a great lob or a long putt loses some of its special richness, but even when playing alone the sense of accomplishment remains. It is a game embraced by participants of all ages, across a wide spectrum of physical well-being, endowed with all levels of skill. It is an activity pursued with a devotion, almost an obsession, by people who may commit an inordinate amount of their energy and time and resources to trying to master it, but who never seem to tire of its hold.

"Never" may sound like a writer's hyperbole, but Dick Emmons, a now deceased reporter for the Ann Arbor News, would not only have agreed, but might even have amended it to "eternity." At his grave site in the Ann Arbor cemetery one can read his epitaph:

> If you should read my tombstone, friend
>
> Here's what will meet your eye:
>
> It isn't dying I resent,
>
> It's this damn buried lie.

And for we seniors, that is the wondrous and all-consuming joy of the game—that it is not just a game for the young or strong or accomplished. As long as we are still ambulatory we can all play golf and play it at varying levels of expertise and continue to get immense pleasure and both physical and psychological benefits from it. The nature of those benefits and pleasures, of course, differs for each of us: for the young athlete it may be the hope of fame or fortune; for the middle-aged "wannabes" it may be the satisfying social encounters; for the older "coulda beens" it may simply be the gratification of still being able to play and the satisfaction of having their game progress even as the rest of their bodies retreat. Or perhaps it is some combination of the three, but the pleasure of playing and competing and constantly improving—to whatever degree, at whatever pace, and at whatever age—remains a powerful source of satisfaction.

Meanwhile, the inventory of older men and women, the pool from which aging golfers may be launched, is growing exponentially larger. Consider, for example, the remarkable statistics emanating from our rapidly increasing longevity: Of all the humans who have ever lived to be 65 years or older, one half are still alive. In the 4,500 years from the Bronze Age to the start of the twentieth century, the longevity of man had increased by about 27 years. In the very brief period from 1900 to the present, however, the average life span has lengthened another 29 years. It may have been that the original 27 additional years of life were only used by our predecessors to improve their chances of survival—catching game or avoiding being caught by game—but the more recent 29 year extension, especially with the advantages bestowed on us by the Social Security Act of 1935, is better characterized by the hunt for leisure-time activities than for dinner table samplings.

A recent MacArthur Foundation study, Successful Aging, a book by John Rowe, M.D. and Robert Kahn, Ph.D., attributes at least part of our increased longevity to our altered and improved lifestyles. Of the authors' three key characteristics for successful aging (the other two being a low risk of disease and a high mental and physical function), the authors claim that the most compelling and essential ingredient, and probably the only one we can still manipulate, is "an active engagement with life." Rowe and Kahn see isolation, on the other hand, as one of the more powerful risk factors for poor health. It is those seniors, they find, who by retiring relinquish the challenges and competition and socialization of the workplace and who then fail to replace them that face the greatest danger to continued health and well-being. That study places a determined emphasis on regular physical activity and a full engagement with life as two of the requisites for successful aging—and to me that sounds a lot like a recipe for golf.

Physical exercise alone, of course, cannot always change our future, but along with a positive and vibrant attitude it can have a mighty impact on the endeavor. And even as old age is an inescapable fact, I enthusiastically embrace the philosophy of Bernard Baruch, the financier and advisor to presidents, who insisted that "To me, old age is always fifteen years older than I am." Clearly, the mere stimulation of physical activities should not be confused with the elixir of life. It will never be enough to recapture a lost youth, nor can it solve such debilitating problems of aging as poverty or ill health, but it does help move its participants out of the damaging malaise of boredom and improve their appetite for using all the hours available to them during each day.

When Homer finished with the adventures of Ulysses he left him back in Ithaca, happy and contented with his kingdom and his wife.

The poet Tennyson, however, in his classic poem "Ulysses," envisioned a different and sadder Ulysses. Ulysses, now an old man, complains

> "How dull it is to pause, to make an end, to rust unburnished, not to shine in use! As though to breathe were life!"

Golf, even great golf, may not be on a par with the adventures recorded in the Odyssey, but it does promise more interest and exercise and engagement with life than the dull existence suffered in old age by Tennyson's Ulysses. And there is a whole army of hackers just like us, who play together and learn together and finally brag over beer together—and that can make for a very satisfying afternoon.

14

ORIGINS OF THE GAME

Legend has it that Romulus and Remus were the founders of the great Roman Empire which finally conquered all its neighbors and extended its influence throughout the entire civilized world. That was a pretty impressive feat for a couple of kids raised by a she-wolf, but the story sells them short. It doesn't give them adequate credit for all they actually accomplished.

Leaving their mark in the field of architecture through the use of the arch—that was good. And the codification of laws really had a big impact on the business of government. And spectator sports, after all, would be nothing today without the gladiators having mixed it up with the lions in their Coliseum.

But the history books completely overlook the immense contribution of the Roman Empire's most civilizing influence on the world—the invention of the game of golf.

Exercising their lust for expanding the empire, the Romans occupied large parts of what is now England and Scotland. After a five-hundred year occupation ending at about 400 A.D., they bestowed upon the newly freed population the glorious gift—considered by some to be the ultimate curse—of a game called "paganica." Little is known about the rules or style of the game except that it was played with a bent stick used to hit a little round ball, made of leather and tightly stuffed with feathers, into a small hole. Somewhere down the road it was renamed "golfe" and adopted by the Scots, who turned it into their national obsession.

And that was the beginning of their trouble. Their other national pastime was doing battle with the English, but the Scots were spending so much time on the course that they had very little time or energy left for archery practice, which in turn threatened their military proficiency. The result was that in 1457 King James II had his parliament pass an act warning the Scotsmen "that fut ball and golfe must be utterly cryit dune." It was soon realized, however, that a complete curtailment would be a bit too restrictive, especially now that royalty and a growing number of noblemen were becoming addicted to the game, so parliament eased its ruling a few years later by merely forbidding the game from being played at any time during the Sabbath. Even that restriction seemed a bit harsh and was soon amended by calling for the prohibition of Sunday golf to just the morning during "sermonses." Who says government has no heart?

But struggles with the devil for custody of the soul are not so easily won. As the Americans learned during the Prohibition of the 1920s, authoritarian demands can't stand up for long against the will of a people and their addictions. And so it was for the Scotsmen, who continued to satisfy their growing and insatiable craving for "golfe," despite parliamentary pressures. The fifteenth-century Scotsman may have been a terror on the battlefield, but he was just not strong enough to quit the game cold turkey, not any more than his American counterpart in the '20s could give up his bathtub gin.

The conflict between the needs of the government and the addiction of the populace continued on its collision course until 1491, when parliament passed a law that not only fixed a fine and imprisonment for anyone caught violating the prohibition, but even punished those who would assist others in satisfying their vile habit. Thank heavens, therefore, for the power of the gentry. The common man may perforce be mute, but if a man of nobility can have no voice in such weighty affairs of state as the pursuit of golfe, then what good is his position. With their influence—and the death of King James in 1513 while trying to invade England—the law was rescinded and the noble Scotsmen resumed their games.

Incidentally, "golfe" was not just a game for men, but proved quite popular with women as well. Mary, Queen of Scots, daughter of the late King James, is said to have swung a mean mashie (similar to today's 7-iron), although she left her imprimatur on the game in quite another way. One of the perks of queenhood was having others carry your clubs, a dividend she accepted enthusiastically, calling her club-carriers her "cadets." The French pronunciation of cadet is "cad-day"—a position still known and honored as "caddie," one which to a large extent has now sadly been replaced by the battery-powered golf cart.

Even as it still is today, the equipment used by the early hotshots was a key factor in their pursuit of excellence, and as it is today that equipment could be very costly. They managed to survive reasonably well without titanium heads or graphite shafts, but the golf ball itself presented an almost insurmountable obstacle in their pursuit of the game. For the first many centuries golf balls were made of strips of leather sewn together to form a ball, then turned inside out to hide the stitching. A small hole was left, through which about a bucket of boiled goose feathers was forcefully injected, using such pressure that the casing almost reached its bursting point. Then the hole was sealed and the finished ball given three coats of paint. The final product (called a "featherie") was not cheap, each one costing the equivalent of about one week's wages. Nor was it very durable. At best, a good ball would last no more than two rounds of play, but even then the shape was no better than transitory, depending on how hard and how well the ball was hit.

Over the course of the years, the featherie, with all its imperfections and some small variations, remained the standard for the industry, but the "great golf ball revolution of 1845" changed all that. That was the year the reverend Dr. Robert Adams Paterson discovered that gutta percha, a packing material used to protect a marble statue of Vishnu shipped to the good Reverend from India, had special properties uniquely applicable to the construction of golf balls. Gutta percha is the juice of a tree native to India and the Far East, a juice that softens in boiling water, then hardens when cooled. While still soft, the gutta percha was placed in molds to insure the desired size and shape, then given two coats of paint and allowed to dry and harden for several weeks. The result was the "guttie," a golf ball that was more uniform than the featherie, much more durable and sold for only a fraction of the featheries' price.

It was not until 1898 that Bertram Work of the B.F. Goodrich Company, a rubber-products manufacturing company in Akron, Ohio, invented the first of what may reasonably be identified as the forerunner of the modern golf ball. The surfaces varied, using different kinds of covering, but its essence was a rubber thread wound tightly around a solid hard-core of rubber.

And so that proud little golf ball, having survived its many earlier transitions, can now take its proper place alongside such other great advances of mankind as the invention of the hockey stick, the squash racquet, and the "fut ball".

15

PLAYING BY THE RULES

If this were a perfect world we would need no rules or regulations. In a perfect world everyone would be reasonable and fair and considerate and the behavior of golfers would be beyond reproach. We would accept gimmies and ignore whiffs and permit Mulligans whenever such actions would boost the morale and add to the joy of our playing partners.

But this is not a perfect world. There are still some people out there who insist on counting it as a stroke every time their opponent swings at the ball, and others who take offense at being penalized a stroke-plus-distance just for hitting out of bounds, and still others who object to being charged a stroke for every ball that has to be fished out of the lake.

It was not always thus. Until the middle of the eighteenth century, "golfe" was a gentlemen's game in which players presumably trusted one another, were considerate toward one another, and where the only disagreements worth noting were likely to be centered on affairs of the British Empire and the health of the queen. Something must have happened in the years preceding 1744, however, because that was the year that The Society of Edinburgh Golfers (later known as The Honorable Company of the Royal and Ancient Club) devised and published the first rules of golf, a list of thirteen do's and don't's to reduce the tension that was beginning to invade the game.

Injecting such formalism into a friendly game of golf played among gentlemen was not a change accepted gracefully. Golf was, after all, the sport of the gentry, built upon camaraderie and good fellowship and more appropriately characterized by another innovation of the game from about that same period—the introduction of the "nineteenth hole," when the game and the day were closed with "copious libations of pure and unadulterated claret."

Inasmuch as golf was a sport engaged in with friends, there was, of course, no need for rules to be complex or oppressive—merely reasonable. In a more recent period, a former United States Golf Association president, Richard Tufts, defined the three basic principles underlying all the rules of the game very simply:

1st—Play the ball as it lies.
2nd—Play the course as you find it.
3rd—When it's not possible to do either, do what's fair.

"...do what's fair." Aye, and therein lies the rub. All too often, fairness is in the eye of the one about to lose a penalty stroke, so it's very helpful to have an objective decision-making process—a published set of rules.

The necessity for the introduction of rules, of course, stemmed from the fact that the game was played under such a wide variety of conditions on fields devoid of uniformity. Inevitably and properly, guidelines for policies and procedures had to emerge from the developing chaos. Those original thirteen rules were rather simple and eminently reasonable decisions on such issues as the propriety of knocking accumulated mud off the ball before hitting it, or relating to the problem of being stymied behind your opponent's ball on the putting green. Unfortunately, unlocking that Pandora's box put a whole new face on the game. The adoption of rules governing propriety and performance was a reasonable response to issues of dispute, but as things changed from those early days of trust between golfers to the necessity in 1744 for the establishment of rules, so have they changed from that day to this. That original short list of rules has since burgeoned into today's prodigious compendium of more than 100 pages.

Nevertheless, to a remarkable degree golf remains a game for gentle-folk, for the men and women who, unlabeled by level of education or wealth or position, are simply united and defined by their character and by the level of their play. It is a game that celebrates camaraderie as much as it promotes a sense of healthy competition and the joy of the outdoors. It is a game of character in which trust and honesty and your relations with your fellow competitors—rather than whether you win or lose—are preeminent. It is a game in which even the blunting force of bad weather offers the alternative pleasures of the nineteenth hole. (I suspect, however, that we may have grown soft with the years, spoiled into succumbing to bad weather too easily. It is the accepted wisdom of the more hearty golfers of Scotland that "If there is nae wind and nae rain, it's nae golf.")

Golf is clearly an honorable game played by people of honor, an affable, if competitive game played among friends. It is a game of character and virtue played by people of character and virtue. And playing by the rules goes a long way toward keeping it that way—or at least in helping maintain that fiction.

RULES OF THE GAME

Long before members of the European Common Market tried to unite their continent with the Eurodollar, even before the term "globalization" gained currency as an economic trend visualizing the whole world as a single field of competition, the stewards of the game of golf saw the need for national and later for international coordination and uniformity. It was after the fiasco in 1894, in which two different tournaments, one at the Newport (Rhode Island) Golf Club and one at St. Andrew's (Scotland) Golf Club, using different sets of rules, yielded two different "National Amateur Champions," that five of the most prestigious golf clubs in the United States joined together to form the Amateur Golf Association of the United States, later to become known as the United States Golf Association (USGA), an umbrella organization charged with setting the rules by which all the separate American golf entities would operate.

The effort was successful and applauded throughout the golf world, so in 1952 the Royal and Ancient Golf Club of St. Andrews (known more familiarly as the "R & A" or "The Old Course," the oldest and most honored entity in the sport) joined with the USGA to devise a single set of rules for golf applicable throughout the world.

◆   ◆   ◆

The organized rules of golf revolve around two types of competition:

> MATCH PLAY, in which each hole is played as a separate and distinct unit of a larger contest. A round of golf may be either nine or eighteen holes and the player who wins the majority number of holes during that round is declared the winner—regardless of the total score.

> STROKE or MEDAL PLAY, in which the winner is that player who uses the lowest number of total strokes to complete the round.

The rules of golf are generally the same for both match and stroke play, but there are instances in which the penalties will necessarily vary. A two-stroke penalty against the player in a stroke play contest, for example, is a very costly burden that must be carried until the end of the game. Those two strokes, after all, will add to his total score and it is the full accumulation of strokes recorded on the scorecard that will determine the winner of the game. In match play, however, inasmuch as each hole is a separate contest, the punishment is concluded at the end of each hole, so the same penalty would have no continuing cost. For that reason, the severity of a stroke play's two-stroke penalty is better matched by a loss-of-hole penalty in a match play contestant.

The single instance in which procedural differences between the two types of play is guided by different rules relates to the offense of a player hitting out of turn. By rights, the player whose ball is farthest from the hole should be the first to hit. If, however, a player should hit out of turn, his opponent in match play may demand that the ball be replayed, but no discipline or penalty is assessed against such a violation in stroke play.

CARE OF THE BALL

- As a general rule, a ball may not be changed during the play of a hole. However, if the ball is damaged during the play of that hole, the opponent may grant permission to use a replacement ball, although such a courtesy is not required.

- If your ball appears to be lost, you are given five minutes from the start of your search to find it. If it cannot be found, you must take a penalty stroke and hit another from the same place from which the lost ball had been hit, finally costing the original stroke, the penalty stroke, and the distance of the original hit.

- If your ball is hit out of bounds (as is generally determined by the local rules and noted on the score card), the same rules as those pertaining to lost balls apply. Having hit your ball, if you are uncertain whether or not it went out of bounds or will be lost (if it goes into the woods, for example, it may or may not have hit a tree and bounced to safety), you may take a "provisional," that is, hit another ball in case the first ball cannot be found. In this way, if the first ball cannot be found, you are saved the time and inconvenience of traveling back to the starting point to hit again. On the other hand, if you find the first ball you may play it and simply pick up the provisional with no penalty.

- Playing the wrong ball can be a very serious offense, incurring a two-stroke penalty in stroke play and causing a forfeit of the hole in match play, so it is obviously of extreme importance that you always know which ball is yours. Given the likelihood of both you and someone else in your foursome using the same brand of golf ball and very possibly the same number, it is highly recommended that you mark your ball in some way to quickly and absolutely identify it as yours. This helps, too, when searching the woods for your otherwise lost ball. Because so many balls are lost in the woods, it is not uncommon to find another that might otherwise be mistaken as your own.

- The only place in which you will not incur a penalty for hitting the wrong ball is in a water or sand hazard, in which case you may replace the ball, then hit your own—without penalty.

LIE OF THE BALL

- You must play the ball as it lies from wherever it finally ends its journey. If it comes to rest in a hazard, such as a bunker or at the edge of a pond or stream, and is so covered with sand or leaves or mud that it cannot be seen, you have the right to remove just enough of the covering necessary to see the ball, but no more. Under no circumstances, however, even to identify the ball as yours, may you lift it or change its position.

- Elsewhere on the course, other than in a sand or water hazard, you may lift the ball in order to identify it as yours (as long as you first notify your opponent of your intention), then replace the ball in as nearly the same spot as possible.

- In the unfortunate case of a ball winding up under a tree or bush without the space to swing a club—sorry 'bout that. You may not bend or break anything growing that happens to be in your way, such as the interfering branch of the pine tree or the six-inch-high weeds enveloping the ball. If you are lucky enough to have the ball stop in the thick grass of the rough just short of the tree, you may lightly ground your club as part of your stance, but you may not press it into the grass behind the ball in order to improve the lie.

- If you have a truly unplayable lie, you may find relief by replacing the ball up to two club-lengths away, but no closer to the hole—but at the cost of a one-stroke penalty.

- It takes no particular skill in lifting and dropping a ball when the rules so allow, but there are parameters within which you must operate. You must put a marker on the spot from which it is being removed, then stand erect with your arm outstretched and drop the ball straight down. If the drop results in the ball rolling onto a section of "ground-under-repair" (which may have been the justification for the "lift-and-drop" in the first place) or some other unacceptable spot, you may drop it again. If after the second drop the situation does not improve, you may simply place it on the spot on which it hit. If on the drop the ball should roll into a hazard (such as a pond or a bunker), you may retrieve it and place it safely away from the hazard by a distance of not more than two club-lengths and no nearer the hole—incurring no penalty.

- The two major categories of obstructions in golf as defined by the USGA are "movable" and "immovable." The definition of movable obstructions are fairly obvious, and include such small man-made items as rakes, cans, bottles—objects that clearly do not belong where they are found and can be moved without much effort—and may be removed without penalty. If the ball should move in the process of removing those obstructions, it may be replaced, again without penalty

    Immovable obstructions include both those of nature that cannot be moved, such as bushes, trees and boulders, all of which are regarded as natural parts of the course, like streams and bunkers and are simply risks to be avoided if possible, and the larger or permanent artificial obstructions that cannot be moved, such as sprinkler heads, equipment shacks, shelters, and cart paths. Relief from immovable natural obstructions carries a penalty, but for artificial immovable obstructions that prove to be a hindrance for striking the ball, penalty-free relief may be granted by dropping the ball to a spot free of interference within a one club-length distance, but not closer to the hole.

There is a single exception to the rule regarding artificial immovable obstructions: fences bordering or defining out-of-bounds limitations are not generally regarded as penalty-free obstructions, so balls hampered by such obstacles may not be granted relief without the cost of a penalty stroke.

- For some situations other than escaping the problems posed by immovable objects, free relief is also available as follows:

  1—If the ball disappears in "casual" water (i.e., a temporary and unplanned accumulation of water such as the result of rain or excessive watering) you may replace the ball along the line of flight from which it entered the water, but no nearer the hole, and take no penalty.

  2—If the ball ends up on the wrong green, you may drop it within one club-length of the green, but not nearer the correct hole, and take no penalty.

  3—If the ball rests in a gopher hole or settles on a spot considered "ground-under-repair," you may, without penalty, either hit it as it lies or take a drop on a straight line between the hole and the place where your ball entered its obstacle, but not closer to the hole.

THE BALL IN MOTION

- Sometimes the ball moves more by accident than by design, in which case it will probably incur a penalty stroke:

    - If the ball is moved by you or your partner—even if by accident—you will be penalized one stroke and the ball must be replaced.

    - If the cause of that movement is the result of someone else's action, such as your opponent or your opponent's caddie, the ball must be replaced, but there will be no penalty stroke.

    - If it is the wind or rain that causes the ball to move, you must play the ball as it currently lies.

    - If the ball falls off the tee without having been touched, just replace it and start again—without a penalty stroke.

- It is not uncommon for a ball to hit the sand trap rake on or near the green or to hit a bird that is still digesting its worm. That is known as the "rub of the green," which seems to be the rough equivalent of "that's the way the ball bounces" or "you win some—you lose some." The result is that you play the ball as it lies, but need incur no penalty.

    If, on the other hand, your ball hits your partner or his bag or your bag or his caddie or yours, you either lose the hole (in match play) or take a two-stroke penalty (in stroke play). If, however, your ball hits your opponent, his caddy, or his bag, there is no penalty—just replay the ball or hit it as it lies. Seems a bit unfair, but that's the rule.

AROUND THE GREEN

- When your ball is in a sand hazard, you may not touch the sand with your club either at the setup or during the backswing. If you find any unnatural objects in the way of your swing, such as bottles or rakes or such extraneous obstructions, you may remove them, but you may not remove any loose natural impediments to your swing, such as twigs and leaves.

- On the putting green, you may use either your hands or your club to remove the leaves and flower petals and twigs and other impediments that may be in the way of your putt, but (for whatever reason) you may not use your towel or hat to fan away that loose debris. It is also permissible to repair ball marks and old hole plugs that may be in the intended path of your ball, but you may not repair scuff marks or indentations from your own shoes or spikes.

- Rolling the ball on the green to determine the speed or the likely break of the putt or scraping your hand over the surface to check the grain of the grass is prohibited.

- When your ball is on the green you may lift it for cleaning or to replace it or to remove it from the line of your opponent's putt, but you must first put a marker behind it.

- When putting from anywhere on the green, the flagstick must be removed from the hole or held by a caddie or another player, to be removed when the ball approaches the hole. If the ball hits the flagstick during the putt, the player will be charged a two-stroke penalty in stroke play or automatically lose the hole in match play. If the ball hits the flagstick when struck from off the green, however (whether putted or chipped), there will be no penalty.

- If you chip or putt from off the green and your ball hits another ball already on the green, you must replace the struck ball and play your own as it lies, but there is no penalty. If you are on the green when you putt, however, and your ball hits another, the other ball must be replaced and you are fined a two-stroke penalty (stroke play) or you lose the hole (match play).

MISCELLANEOUS

- In these days of the proliferation of types and hypes of equipment in which the simple pitching wedge has been joined by a range of loft wedges boasting face angles up to 62 degrees, and collections of fairway woods numbering all the way through the 12-wood, and with assortments of drivers that now include heads ranging from "big" heads to "bigger" heads to "jumbo" heads to "monstrous" heads, etc., you should be aware of a seldom-noticed rule (of potential significance) that limits each player to just fourteen clubs. Fortunately, that limitation excludes the ball retriever (a device used for the recovery of errant shots from watery graves) and an umbrella.

- You may practice swinging your club whenever and wherever you wish, but no practice shots are allowed during play. (A fairly common, but very unprofessional variance, is the acceptance of the "mulligan," a free second drive on the first hole, but you'd better get advance agreement from the rest of the foursome before taking that second shot.)

- Drives must be hit from between the tee markers or from up to two club-lengths behind the marker, but never from in front.

◆　　　◆　　　◆

The rules of golf were written to maintain structure and harmony in the game, and apply equally to the professionals playing for prestigious titles and big bucks, to the amateurs playing for their club championship, and to those weekend warriors whose goal simply includes escaping the tensions of their workday responsibilities. Some of us less accomplished players, however, may find some of the rules to be just a bit too confining and intractable for our taste.

Okay, then change them. There is no law that says the rules cannot be bent or redesigned to fit the needs and accommodate the moods of Sunday swingers—as long as agreement is reached beforehand. For example, the rules state unequivocally that there will be no "gimmies" (putts so short they need not be stroked into the hole). This is a good rule on the perfectly reasonable grounds that they eliminate unpleasant and unnecessary arguments. What seems to be an obvious "gimmie" for one player, after all, may appear to be an obstacle-strewn pathway to his opponent. For a sociable game among friends, however, there may well be an unstated understanding that the opponent simply calls the other's short putt a "gimmie" and goes on to the next hole. A safer arrangement, however, may be an advance agreement to forgive any additional putt that falls "within the leather,"that distance of the ball from the cup that is measured by the clubhead to the lower edge of the putter's grip.

Another formal rule at odds with the flavor of a friendly game of golf regards the prohibition of seeking and giving advice. According to the accepted United States Golf Association's Rules of Golf, you may not ask anyone except your caddie or your partner about how a hole should be played, nor are you permitted to give such advice to your opponent. Even for rank amateurs, this rule is not such a bad idea. Weekend foursomes often include one player who feels he has the answer to your slice or your bunker problems or who knows the vagaries of the course and is anxious to pass his wisdom on to you. Not surprisingly, such unsolicited advice can be annoying, tiresome or just plain wrong. It is probably a good idea to keep such self-anointed instructors from inflicting their advice on you, but simply not listening or the admonition to "be quiet" will probably suffice, and avoiding the tensions of even a minor confrontation does make the nineteenth hole a much more pleasurable experience.

And that's the point. At our age and with our skills, golf should be fun and any of the restrictions that reduce our enjoyment of the game should be analyzed, rethought, and probably discarded.

16

VARIATIONS IN THE GAME

or
Adding Dollars to the Glory

The overriding goals of golf are to improve your game and achieve consistently low scores, but one of the other pleasures of the game (ah, the joys of small sins) is betting and beating your opposition. The obvious bet—that your score will be lower than his or hers—will generally suffice to divide your small world into one of well-defined winners and losers, but a prolonged losing streak may drive you to seek newer and more novel contests.

The desperation that drives such competitive ploys is the hope that by changing the rules or options or lingo of the game it will somehow encourage the fates or the hidden demons of golf to reverse their curse and favor you with their blessings. It has much in common with knocking on wood or crossing your fingers or buying a lottery ticket—and with much the same predictable outcome. Nevertheless, some of us keep on trying—and hoping—and losing.

Meanwhile, however hopeless our quest, we have plenty of support for alternatives to the standard rules by which we have been losing. There are now enough combinations and permutations flying around within and between foursomes that the challenge for today's competitive golfer has moved beyond selecting the right club and properly reading the green. It now includes knowing what game you're playing and memorizing its complex rules.

In brief, golf is no longer simply the "golfe" of the 15th century King James. It may now be "Scramble" or "Wolfman" or "Bingo, Bango, Bongo" or any one of the many variations that are described below:

The two generally accepted standards of competitive golf are

MEDAL PLAY or STROKE PLAY

This is the traditional game of golf, picked up and polished by the Scots in the year 1100. It is rumored to have been copied from a game left behind by the Romans when they ended their occupation of England and Scotland at about several hundred AD—when greens fees were considerably lower. The game is straightforward and basic—the low total score (i.e., the lowest number of strokes charged to the scorecard) wins the competition.

MATCH PLAY

This, too, has a tradition, but it probably dates from a period long after the golf balls of leather stuffed with feathers were replaced by gutta percha, the solidified milky juice of a Malaysian gutta tree. In this competition, the player who has won the greater number of holes is the winner.

Whether the play is medal or match, however, the condition common to both is the will to victory, the goal of defeating your opponent on this green field of battle. Of course the games must be played within the rules governing medal and match play, but none of the rules is so rigid that it cannot be revised by common consent. As is true in politics and religion and social customs, after all, traditions have a long tradition of being broken, supplemented, or supplanted. Nevertheless, some of the more common contests in competitive golf are listed below:

NASSAU

This is the most popular betting game in golf and perhaps the easiest to apply. It is match play between two golfers wherein the front nine holes are played as one match, the back nine are played as a second match and all eighteen holes are considered a third match. An optional fourth match is a "press" between the nines. This is an additional bet that gives the loser of the front nine the advantage of half the difference of the front-nine loss as his handicap for the back nine. In other words, if one player lost the front nine by five holes, he goes into the back nine already two and one-half holes ahead on the new bet. Because these bets are determined by the number of holes won or lost, Nassau is pretty well limited to match play competition.

PRESS

This is a wager that is generally only used in Nassau and must be initiated by the player who is losing, usually by a minimum of two holes. It is an extra bet that begins on the hole at which the bet is made, but exists only for the balance of that nine. For example, if a press is demanded at the start of the sixth hole, it remains in effect for only the next four holes, and is complete at the end of the nine. Another press may become available when the losing player is two or more strokes behind the previous press. If agreed to in advance, an "automatic press" (as defined in "Nassau" above) may be called for to become operative at the end of the first nine holes.

BINGO, BANGO, BONGO

This is a good game for leveling out the disadvantages of a high handicap. Three points are available on each hole: One for the first player's ball to reach and remain on the green, one for the ball closest to the pin once all the balls are on the green, and one for the first player to hole out. Even if the poorer player requires several strokes more than his competitors to get there, being on the green first wins the point—which makes the game more dependent on luck than on skill, much to the advantage of the less qualified player. The player with the most points at the end of the round wins the competition.

HIGH SCORE

Although the name is somewhat misleading, this is a good game for a threesome. Each hole is worth twelve points—six for the lowest score, four for the second lowest, and two for the highest. In case of ties, the available points are split. For example, if two players are tied for low, the ten points for low and second are split, giving five to each. As with Bingo, Bango, Bongo, the player with the most points at the end of the round wins the competition.

PLAY IT AGAIN, SAM

This is a method of play that utilizes the handicap system, but somewhat in reverse. Instead of the higher-handicapped player reducing his score by the difference of the total handicaps of the two players, any player in this game may demand that his opponent take his shot over. The number of times that demand may be exercised is determined by the number of handicap strokes the challenged player is allowed. For example, an opponent's great drive or outstanding pitch may be nullified by the use of the "play it again, Sam" option, an action that may be used as many times as the handicap difference allows.

I PLAY AGAIN

This is essentially the same as "Play It Again Sam," except that the handicap determines the time and number of mulligans that a player may use for himself rather than as a punishment for his opponent. If the difference between the two players' handicaps is four, for example, the higher handicapped player may choose any four shots as his mulligans.

SCRAMBLE

This is a format commonly used for tournament play. Teams may consist of two pairs of players within a foursome or of all four members of a foursome playing against other foursomes. Beginning with the drive, each player on a team hits the ball, then the lie of the best ball is used by all members of that team for the next shot. Each member of the team places his ball within a club-length of the ball selected to be played, then each hits his second shot. Once again, the best shot of the four is chosen and the procedure is repeated still again (including putts), until the final putt of the hole is sunk.

SKINS

This is a form of wager made popular by the televised tournaments of the professional golfers. Each "skin" is worth a certain dollar amount and is won for each hole by the player with the lowest total score on that hole. In case of a tie, the bet is carried over to the next hole, making that hole worth double the amount, and so on until there is a winner. When more than two players are in the contest, the carryover applies to all players.

STABLEFORD

This is another popular format for match play tournaments, and works particularly well in taking into account handicap differences. Point values are assigned to the various scores, such as a bogey being worth one point, a par worth two points, a birdie worth three points, an eagle worth four points and a double-eagle worth five points. If a player's handicap allows him a stroke on an upcoming par four hole, for example, and he actually scores a par on that hole, then his net score of a birdie-three rewards him (according to the point values agreed above) with three points.

GREENIES

This is a competition that applies only to par-three holes. The potential winner must reach and hold the green with his drive. If two or more players reach the green on the drive, the point (or win) belongs to the one nearest the hole. In order to win the greenie, however, the selected player (the one who drove the green and was closest to the hole) must make par or the greenie is forfeited. Variations in the rules exist, such as permitting carryovers, but must be determined in advance.

WOLF

"Wolf," like many of the games included in this section, is a game of many variations, but most of the variations are in the manner of the scoring. Essentially, the game is a competition between two teams of two players each, the makeup of the two teams changing with each hole. The lead-off driver on each hole is the Wolfman for that hole. Immediately after each of the other players hits his drive the Wolfman must decide whether or not he wants that player as his partner for that hole. In other words, he must take or reject Player #2 as his partner before Player #3 hits his drive, and so on. The position of the Wolfman in the lineup alternates with each hole, each player taking his turn on succeeding holes. For each hole the winning team is the one whose member has the lowest score for that hole, regardless of the other high or low scores.

If he desires, the Wolfman may go it alone, choosing to take no partners for that hole, in which case he stands to win from all three opponents. The potential payoff in the event he wins can be fairly seductive, but the risk can be rather daunting, inasmuch as a loss or a tie costs the Wolfman double the bet. In the event of a carryover of one or more of the previous holes, such a loss can threaten to make the Wolfman a very endangered species.

BEST BALL

In the game of "Best Ball," each team of two players will simply play their own game with their own ball. The lower score of the two members of the team will be recorded as the team's score for the hole, and the final one-total per hole overall score will determine the winning team for that hole. This game is equally applicable for match or stroke play competition.

LOW BALL—LOW TOTAL

Unlike "Best Ball" team play, wherein the lowest score wins the hole for his team, "Low Ball—Low Total" awards one point for the low scoring ball and another point for the team with the lower total score for the hole. In this way, players who are out of the running for the low score still have a part to play by keeping their high score low enough to help with the low total.

LOW BALL—HIGH BALL

This is essentially the same as "Low Ball—Low Total," except that instead of bringing the poorer scoring players into the game by adding both scores of each team together to find the low team score, one point is deducted for the higher score on each hole. Thus, the team with the lower score on each hole wins one point, while the individual with the highest score on each hole loses a point for his team. Obviously, many holes break even, as partners may score both low ball and high ball between them.

And then there is SNAKE, THE WORST OF TWO, SIX-SIX-SIX, TRASH, VEGAS, FLAG DAY, STRING, FOUR OF CLUBS...and the list goes on...and on...and on. The variations of the games are as numerous as the dimples on the golf ball—and they are not for everyone. Classicists embrace the purity of the game and disdain the pollution these variations bring to it. Others, having nothing to do with golf, simply enjoy a wager—like those people who bet on which of two flies will leave the windowpane first. The fact is that golf is about competition—whether against oneself or against a single opponent or as a member of a team against other teams—and simply the satisfaction of competing successfully can be quite fulfilling. The nature and the basis for that satisfaction varies with the individual, but for those who seek the added spice of a small wager, there are more than enough betting alternatives from which to choose to keep them on their toes.

17

DEMOGRAPHICS

or
Who We Are

The perks of civilization keep upgrading. Our forefathers may have been satisfied simply with securing a reliable shelter from the elements, and a later generation may have been thrilled with the addition of indoor plumbing, but today's residential demands include easy access to a nearby golf course. The 17,108 golf courses in our nation's inventory in the year 2000, still increasing at the rate of about 400 new courses each year, would appear to satisfy that demand.

The growth of the golf industry in this country is staggering. The number of players has grown from 19.9 million golfers in 1986 to 26.7 million in 2000, while their golf-related expenditures have increased even more dramatically—inflating from $7.8 billion to $22.2 billion during that same period.

And leading that charge are the senior players, who as a group are in better physical and financial shape than those of any previous generation. Our health system and health habits, for example, enable older Americans to participate in leisure-time activities much more fully than in any of the preceding senior populations. Even more significant, however, is the impact on the industry of the growing number of those senior players who, beside simply living longer and stronger, are now enjoying the benefits of Social Security and of retirement plans that are increasingly available to both white-and blue-collar workers, giving them both the time and the disposable income to actively and confidently pursue their pleasures.

In the wake of that interest has come a host of consumer products to feed the expanding appetite. The mashies and brassies and niblicks of just a few years ago have given way to metal woods and jumbo woods and titanium heads and graphite shafts. Even the golf balls have had the number and size of their dimples increased and endlessly rearranged in an effort to achieve greater loft or longer distance.

What is surprising, however, is the limited attention focused on the older players. The public library in my hometown of Ann Arbor, Michigan, for example, has 103 books about golf, ranging in focus from "How To…" to "Where To…" to "With What," but nothing at all for senior amateurs. (Of greater significance was the inventory at amazon.com before they changed their method of maintaining book inventory records. Its available titles then included 4,461 books related to golf, only four of which were designed for older hackers…and two of those were out of print.)

The purpose of including this statistical section in the book is to give aid and comfort to those seniors who may have missed the boat (or in this case, the golf cart) in gaining some early level of proficiency in the game, and to casual players who have never progressed beyond terrible, and to non-players who are trying to catch up to terrible. It is an attempt to reach and reassure those sidelined seniors that it's not too late to start, to let them know that being a few decades beyond their prime has not cost them all their options. The statistical tables that follow should convince them that there is yet time to review and discard some of those outdated clichés that categorize aging seniors as helpless or hopeless. A study of the following pages will make clear that those enthusiastic neophytes, however ancient, are not alone in their belated efforts nor is their cause hopeless. There are many players in the senior age group struggling to get around the course, players whose scores number closer to their cholesterol count than to their age. but who nevertheless profit enormously from the experience.

The statistical tables provided here by the National Golf Foundation are surprising and deserve some study. For example, in the year 2000, over 27 percent of the 26,738,000 golfers in the United States, 7,249,000 players, classify as seniors. That number represents an increase of 28.1 percent in just the last five years. Equally surprising is the fact that over 38 percent of those included in this senior category—a total of 2,760,000 golfers—are 65 years old or older. One reassuring figure revealed by these statistics examines the expertise of those senior golfers relative to their juniors. I had assumed that golfers still playing at age 60 or more, presumably after having played and practiced for at least several decades, must by now be pretty well accomplished. I was pleased and reassured to learn that my ineptitude did not make me truly unique—merely inadequate.

The problem with these statistics is that the category of "senior golfer" begins with players aged only 50, which is almost insulting to those of us aged 70 or beyond. These statistics reveal that most golfers in the "Senior" classification are well into their 60s and have been playing the game for the better part of three decades—and are still unable to break 100. As a group, incidentally, we play much more golf than do our juniors—almost three times as much. We play about 40 rounds of golf per year as compared to the 14 rounds played by the average player of non-senior status.

I realize, of course, that age is a relative condition of life, not a precise and finite measurement that defines ability or behavior. Nevertheless, I was a bit uneasy having it thrown in my face (inadvertently, of course) by some of the youngsters who worked in my travel agency just before my retirement several years ago. I became aware of a party of sorts taking place in the lunch room at noon and asked one of the young ladies what it was all about.

"Oh, we're having a birthday party...for me!" she announced proudly. Then, and with some sense of awe at the terrible reality of it all, she exclaimed "It's my big three-O!"

At any rate, it's nice to know there are so many older, optimistic golfers still active in the game, and so many more who are just now taking up the game at an advanced age…and with still a lot of room and potential to grow and to improve. And it's nice to know that, at whatever age, it is likely that we'll still be able to find a foursome.

Meanwhile, you are welcome to use the following pages of assorted statistics to arrive at your choice of conclusions. It was the British Prime Minister Benjamin Disraeli, after all, who once recognized the three levels of untruths as "lies, damn lies—and statistics." By using the National Golf Foundation's statistics you may be able to escape unfair charges of extravagance by showing that your golf expenses are less than that of most people your age. Or perhaps you can use them to convince your family that although not yet as good as you are going to be, you are better than the average of your peers. Or maybe you can use them to con your housemate into believing that you only seem to be spending an inordinate amount of time on the golf course, that it's perfectly in line with the average of seniors nationwide.

However you wish to view and twist the facts, the statistics are all here—for the lies and damn lies you're on your own.

18

Statistical Tables

DEMOGRAPHIC PROFILE OF U.S. GOLFERS—2003

Population	Number of Golfers (thousands)	Percent all Golfers
Total	**27,400**	**100.0%**
Gender		
Male	20,769	75.8%
Female	6,631	24.2%
Age		
18-29 yrs.	5,179	18.9%
30-39 yrs.	6,850	25.0%
40-49 yrs.	6,960	25.4%
50-59 yrs.	4,000	14.6%
60-64 yrs.	1,397	5.1%
65 and over	3,014	11.0%
Household Income		
Under $20,000	1,754	6.4%
$20,000-29.999	1,836	6.7%
$30,000-39,999	2,548	9.3%
$40,000-49.999	2,438	8.9%
$50,000-74,999	6,412	23.4%

DEMOGRAPHIC PROFILE OF U.S. GOLFERS—2003 (Continued)

$75,000-99,999	5,288	19.3%
$100,000 and over	7,124	26.0%

Education (Head of Household)

Non-HS Grad	665	2.5%
HS Grad	4,603	16.8%
Some College	9,823	32.2%
College Grad	13.289	48.5%

Occupation (Head of Household)

Prof/Mgt/Adm	11,261	41.1%
Clerical/Sales	4,274	15.6%
Blue Collar	6,220	22.7%
Other	1,945	7.1%
Retired/not Employed	3,699	13.5%

DEMOGRAPHIC PROFILE OF SENIOR GOLFERS-2003

Population	Participation Rate % of population age 50+	Number of Golfers (thousands)	% Senior Golfers
Total	**10.9%**	**8,412**	**100.0%**
Gender			
Male	12.1%	6,006	71.4%
Female	5.8%	2,406	28.6%

DEMOGRAPHIC PROFILE OF SENIOR GOLFERS-2003 (Continued)

Age

50-59 yrs.	11.3%	3,979	47.3%
60-64 yrs.	12.9%	1,590	18.9%
65-69 yrs.	11.1%	1,237	14.7%
70 and over	7.3%	1,607	20.1%

Household Income

Under $20,000	3.3%	598	7.1%
$20,000-29.999	6.4%	669	8.0%
$30,000-39,999	8.6%	802	9.5%
$40,000-49.999	9.2%	587	7.0%
$50,000-74,999	12.0%	1,507	17.9%
$75,000-99,999	14.8%	1,466	17.4%
$100,000 and over	23.5%	2,782	33.1%

Education

Non-HS Grad	1.9%	218	2.6%
HS Grad	1.8%	1,287	15.3%
Some College	9.4%	2,751	32.7%
College Gad	10.5%	4,156	49.4%

Occupation

Prof/Mgt/Adm	19.4%	2,860	34.0%
Clerical/Sales	18.1%	841	10.0%
Blue Collar	9.4%	1,127	13.4%

DEMOGRAPHIC PROFILE OF SENIOR GOLFERS-2003 (Continued)

Other	9.2%	353	4.2%
Retired/not Employed	10.5%	3,230	38.4%

SENIOR GOLFER AVERAGES

VARIATIONS WITHIN DIFFERENT CLASSIFICATIONS

ALL SENIOR GOLFERS (2003)

Age	61.6
Household Income	$84,580
Annual Rounds Played	33.6

CORE (AVID) SENIOR GOLFERS (2003)

Age	62.4
Household Income	$87,520
Annual Rounds Played	50.6

COMPARISONS (2003)

	SENIOR GOLFERS	OTHER ADULT GOLFERS
Age	50+	18-49
Household Income	$84,580	$76,520

VARIATIONS WITHIN DIFFERENT CLASSIFICATIONS (Continued)

Annual Rounds Played	36.6	12.4
Household spending on Golf (including fees and equipment)	$1,690	$991

SENIOR GOLFER PROFILE

	Senior Golfers	All Other Golfers
Number of Golfers	6.2 million	16.8 million
Total Rounds Played	229.1 million	233.2 million
Average Age	62.4 years	34.1 years
Average Income	$56,300	$56,600
Average # rounds played last 12 months	36.7	13.9
Played golf 1-7 times last year	31.0%	56.6%
Played golf 8-24 times last year	24.1%	27.2%
Played golf 25 or more times last year	44.9%	16.2%
Average number of years played	26.2	11.5
Average age when started	36.1	22.7
% of rounds played at public facilities	72.8%	80.7%
Average 18 hole score the past year	101.4	99.9
Maintain a handicap	28.9%	12.7%
Average current handicap	20.5	15.7
% that plays 9 hole rounds	37.2%	39.6%
% that plays 18 hole rounds	62.1%	59.1%
% that plays more than 18 hole rounds	0.7%	1.4%
% of rounds played on a regulation course	83.7%	82.4%
% of rounds played on an executive course	4.5%	2.7%

SENIOR GOLFER PROFILE (Continued)

% of rounds played on a par 3 course	8.0%	8.9%
Average # times used a driving range last year	2.3	3.1
Annual expenditure on all golf-related items	$939	$625
Annual expenditure on golfing fees	$680	$414
Annual expenditure on equipment/merchandise	$332	$266
Lives within a golf-oriented development	16.6%	14.5%
Owns or rents a residence within a golf-oriented development	4.8%	2.8%
Owns investment property in a golf-oriented development	4.0%	1.7%

The Nature and Range
of
INVOLVEMENT IN GOLF

*Responses from those golfers who
answered "often" or "sometimes" to
those catagories listed below:*

	Senior Golfers	All Other Golfers
	%	%
Watch golf on television	82	64
Read golf-related magazines	50	31
After the round, I remember each shot	53	53
Try new golf equipment	46	37
Will buy new club if I think it will help my game	46	34
Make bets while playing golf	32	30
Take golf lessons	22	18
Compete in golf tournaments	38	26

Willing to make a financial sacrifice to play golf	36	25
Willing to play golf in bad weather	39	34
Work on my game at a practice facility	30	40
Take golf vacations	23	13
Daydream about golf while at work	20	23

19

THE EQUIPMENT

or

Tools of the Trade

The science that put man into space is now trying to do the same for the golf ball, albeit in a somewhat lower orbit, and it seems to be succeeding. In just the last few years space-age materials and techniques have begun providing golfers and golf equipment manufacturers with options and aspirations that until a few years earlier were not even within the range of fantasy. The beginning of the end for the universally accepted all-wood clubhead, for example, began only a few decades ago when Taylor-Made introduced its first metal woods. Then, in 1973, the graphite shaft showed up as a more expensive but highly preferable alternative to the old heavier steel (which in turn had earlier replaced the wooden shaft), and then in 1991 Callaway's oversized wood, the Big Bertha, appeared, becoming the most successful golf club in history Even today's most common and widely used putter, the center-shafted putter (so-called because the shaft connects to the center of the putter head rather than to the end) has only been legal for tournament play since 1951.

The game of golf may be almost as old as civilization, but many of its more important innovations are not much older than our grandchildren.

Along with the technology that defines them, the names of the clubs have changed as well. The colorful individuality of clubs that had once been identified as mashie and brassie and niblick has unfortunately given way to the current cold and impersonal numbering system, so books on golf printed earlier than a few decades ago will be as confusing and obscure as Old English epic poetry.

Following are the outdated names and their modern-day equivalents for the most commonly carried golf clubs:

THE WOODS

- The longnose or the play club was the earlier name of today's driver.

- The brassie, used on the fairway, is the equivalent of today's 2-wood. (The name derives from the brass sole-plate intended to protect the clubhead from being damaged when slammed into the ground at the bottom of the swing.)

- The long spoon is comparable to the 3-wood, and...

- The short spoon or the baffy is today's 4-wood. Both the long and short spoons were designed primarily for use in the shallow rough bordering the fairway or for shorter fairway shots.

THE IRONS

- The 1-iron was known as the cleek or the driving iron, and as the name implies, was meant for driving or for long fairway shots

- The 2-iron was known as the midiron.

- The 3-iron was called the mid-mashie.

- The 4-iron was called the mashie iron.

- The 5-iron was simply the mashie.

- The 6-iron was the spade mashie.

- The 7-iron was the mashie niblick.

- The 8-iron was the pitching niblick.

- The 9-iron was the niblick or the track iron.

But that was yesterday, when players drove to the course in their Pierce-Arrows or Stutz-Bearcats (or Model T Fords for the less affluent members) and gave their clubs to the caddies in preparation for tee-off. Times change and the world moves on. Some of those fine old golfing traditions have long since gone the way of the featherie and the guttie, and ordering a spoon or mashie from your pro shop today is more likely to get you a luncheon menu than a golf club. On the other hand, for those who can rise above the romance and nostalgia for days long past, the advantages of the improved quality and performance of the current equipment offer the potential for greatly improved play for the amateur and professional alike.

The treasured hickory and persimmon driving and fairway woods have been replaced by laminated wood or by metal or by one of the new metallic composites such as titanium. The new alloys tend to be lighter in weight, allowing for the construction of a larger than normal clubhead, which in turn provides a larger and more accommodating hitting area, or "sweet spot." Among its other advantages, the larger sweet spot promises to reduce the likelihood of hitting slices or hooks by striking the ball more cleanly on the club's face.

Considered to be even more important than the clubhead, however, is the material and design of the shaft. Since the demise of the wood shaft in 1929, the most commonly used materials are steel, still the least expensive and most durable; graphite, introduced in 1973, more expensive but lighter and with less vibration; and now Titanium, the most expensive and most stiff.

Because the material used in the shaft has a specific role to play, choosing just one from among the several alternatives depends on the preference and performance of the player. The strong player with a fast swing, for example, has better results with a stiff shaft because it keeps the clubhead from lagging behind the shaft when coming back down into the ball. Slower swingers (a category that includes most older golfers) tend to profit from that lag, so they generally do better with a light weight, highly flexible shaft, benefiting from the extra "kick" that comes from the clubhead suddenly catching up to the shaft at about the time of contact with the ball.

Another variation in the design of the shaft that has a serious role to play is the "flex point" (also known as the "kick point" or "bend point"). As the name implies, this is the place on the shaft that exhibits the greatest flexibility under the pressure of a hard swing—the higher flex point (which simulates the effect of a stiff shaft) results in a lower trajectory of the ball, while the lower flex point (mirroring the style of a soft shaft) allows for a higher trajectory.

The industry has not yet come out with a specially designated line of clubs for older golfers, but there are nevertheless a number of important details for a senior players to consider when choosing from among the current crop of woods and irons. For example, Barney Adams of Adams Golf, the manufacturer of the Tight Lies clubs, suggests that seniors, because of the more limited clubhead speed they are able to invoke, carry no irons longer than a 5-or 6-iron, insisting that shots requiring more distance than that can be better accommodated by the more lofted 7-or 9-woods, an attitude generally shared by many pros and most other club manufacturers as well. Adams also likes the flexible graphite shaft for older players for the same reason, seeing value in the "whip" of a clubhead as it comes into the ball after having lagged behind the shaft on its journey down from the peak of the backswing.

Keeping in mind the importance of the short game, particularly for older players who can no longer rely on the power of their long game to gain much yardage on the fairway, the various short clubs have a particularly valuable role to play. To satisfy the expanded need for accuracy, a range of wedges has been developed to provide choices to fit most situations and preferences, including the following (for purposes of comparison, know that the 9-iron has a face with a 44 degree loft):

The pitching wedge, which has a 48 degree loft.

The gap wedge, so-called because it fills the gap between the pitching wedge and the sand wedge, has a 52—53 degree loft.

The sand wedge and its 56 degree loft (and its heavy flange to keep from digging into the sand).

The lob wedge, designed with a 58—60 degree loft.

The problem is that the official Rules of Golf, adopted by the USGA (United States Golf Association) and the R & A (Royal and Ancient Golf Club of St. Andrews, Scotland) restricts the number of clubs carried in a bag to a total of 14 (a limitation not usually recognized in games among friends but vigorously enforced in tournament play and in grudge matches between ex-friends), so we should examine our preferences and tailor our choice of clubs to our individual levels of strength and skill. Following the recommendations of Adams and most other better golf club manufacturers, for example, seniors should replace the 3-iron and 4-iron with a 7-wood and a 9-wood. The new small-headed metal-wood (labeled the "Rescue" club when introduced by Taylor-Made, although now available from other manufacturers under other names) has lofts of 18 and 21 degrees. This has special value in hitting out of the rough or for replacing the 3-iron when a long, low shot is needed to escape the overhanging branches of intervening trees.

Another possible victim of your club-reduction program could be the driver. Although we all aspire to the dazzling long drive, it sometimes comes into conflict with our need for tighter control. Accordingly, a number of seniors and fairly accomplished amateurs alike find that the longer shaft of the driver allows for too many errors when trying to take full advantage of its potential, so they prefer driving with the 3-wood, finding security and improved performance with its shorter and more manageable shaft.

With a collection, then, of the driver or the 9-wood, and the 3-, 5 and 7-woods plus the Rescue club, the putter, and the 5-through 9-irons, we may then decide which one of the four choices of wedges to eliminate in order to keep within the 14 club limit—a decision that falls on each player according to his/her preference. On the other hand, of course, we can include all four wedges, the driver, the 4-iron and even add a ball retriever—and just not enter any major tournaments.

The grip may also be made of various materials, although none of their differences are terribly significant. In days of yore they were always made of leather, soft, comfortable, and possessed of a certain "tackiness" to help maintain a good traction. Another grip is made of rubber or a rubber composite, which works just fine and is probably the cheapest grip available. The third grip material is cord, which has the benefit of offering the best adhesion in the case of rain or from sweating on a hot summer day. One small consideration when contemplating a new grip is the size of the grip for your hands; a grip too small tends to increase the likelihood of a hook, while a grip too large could lead to a slice. More important than the material, however, is the choice of a construction that makes it more comfortable and manageable for players suffering from arthritic hands. These enlarged grips are not very expensive (only a few dollars each) and are available from all golf club manufacturers and most golf shops.

The most significant factor when considering new clubs, however, has little to do with science or price or reputation. It is the "feel" of the club in the hands of the player, an instinctive, subjective evaluation that does not yield to logic or to the realities of weight or balance. All you can do when making this very expensive, long-lived decision is to try as many different clubs as you reasonably can, thereby making a choice based on at least some level of experience—then hope you don't find it to have been a mistake later on.

Meanwhile, it makes little sense to study the unique characteristics of the shaft and the clubhead and the many other features of the modern golf club without an adequate understanding of the object toward which the scientific redesign of the equipment is directed—the golf ball itself.

Not surprisingly, all golf balls are not alike. The number, arrangement, and depth of those surface dimples are not simply decorative but are major factors in determining the flight of the ball—how high it flies, how far it travels, how much and what kind of spin is generated. The very fact of dimples, incidentally, grew out of the realization by an earlier generation of golfers that the older balls, complete with nicks and scuffs, flew better than their new, perfectly smooth, mint-conditioned brothers, that their flight was favorably affected by the turbulence caused by their imperfections. Studies show that the aerodynamics of that contrived, dimpled surface may send a ball 300 yards, while the same force applied to a smooth ball would propel it no more than 100 yards. Even the specifications of those dimples vary according to the objective of the manufacturer: providing greater or less spin, achieving greater or less height, encouraging or restricting the amount of roll after landing. The dimples may even be reconfigured or reformulated with differing degrees of depression in order to better direct the airflow above and below the ball for maximum flight control. And then again we may prefer the balls designed with 432 icosahedral dimples as opposed to those with 392 octahedrals...or whatever—all mysterious designations understood by only a select few.

On the other hand, you don't really have to understand the abstruse science of golf ball construction in order to drive it down the fairway, not any more than you must understand the mechanics of the internal combustion engine to drive your car down the highway. (I'm reminded of the time in my childhood when my very old, immigrant grandfather was struggling—still again—to get a driver's license. For the exam question about the purpose of the muffler, his answer was, "To keep me warm in winter." He was a fine grandfather, but he never did get his driver's license.) It is enough simply to be aware of the remarkable application and achievement of the science that went into the design of the golf ball and to appreciate the technology that guides the golf ball's performance—when you don't screw it up.

But even if you cannot fully comprehend the nature of the leading-edge technologies that are incorporated in golf ball design, it is important that you have enough understanding of the construction of the golf ball to be able to choose the best ball for your particular game. And those differences in golf ball construction really can make a difference—even at our amateur level of play.

There are two broad categories in the structure of the golf ball. The "wound ball," the industry standard until recently, is one in which rubber thread is wound around either a liquid-filled core or a solid core of synthetic rubber. It tends to have good spin control but at the expense of distance. The "solid ball," introduced in the 1980s and rapidly replacing the wound ball, includes three different constructions: one-piece balls, made of a single synthetic rubber core; two-piece balls, in which the center core is itself encased in an outer layer of a urethane resin, which is referred to as the second core or "mantle", each core having different and complementary properties in order to provide a broader range of benefits; and the multi-layer (three-piece) balls, in which two different urethane resins are used to make possible still more options of flight. All of this is then encased in a white dimpled shell, usually made of surlyn, a plastic covering designed to withstand most of the cuts and abrasions inflicted by hard swinging golf clubs.

Here again, a solid comprehension of the scientific details of the alternative constructions are not necessary to your game, but understanding the ways in which these variations respond to your particular swing are important, for which the following abbreviated explanation of the physics of propulsion may be of value:

When the clubhead comes into contact with the ball, the ball itself is flattened (deformed) for a brief instant. The condition of coming out of that flattened or deformed state is called "restitution," and it is in the physics of that restitution that the power of the stroke is manifested. It is almost like we're given a second shot at it—the original explosion of the clubhead striking the ball, followed by the power generated by the restitution or the reformulation of the ball as it regains its original spherical shape. Very briefly, the greater the deformation and subsequent restitution, the greater the velocity of the ball as it leaves the clubhead, all of which varies according to the structure and materials used in its manufacture. Which in its essence simply means that we need not swing with all our might in order to make our mark.

Our problem, given the many variables built into all the different kinds of golf balls on the market, is to determine which is best for our particular needs. Until recently, "compression", the measurement defining how much a golf ball deforms when impacted by the club, was the criterion by which distance could be forecast. The theory was that a lower compression ball provided the optimum deformation and restitution of the golf ball when struck by a slower moving club. Unfortunately, the myriad innovations recently launched by the industry has introduced a whole new set of criteria, most of which are beyond the comprehension of the lay public and as well as most professionals. Many manufacturers no longer even provide information on the compression of their golf balls, forcing the buyer instead to rely for a clue to the ball's construction on the murky pictures or obscure jargon appearing on each box of new balls. Nevertheless, we can get some sense of anticipated performance from Precept, the only golf ball manufacturer to make a ball specifically marketed for Seniors, and compare it to some of their other balls.

For comparative purposes, their ball for low-handicap heavy-hitters carries a compression of about 90 psi (pounds per square inch), whereas the Ladies ball has a compression of about 65 psi and the Senior ball, a compression of about 60 psi. The good news, then, is that if our favorite brand of golf ball does not carry a "Senior" label, and if we cannot find a ball that identifies its compression as about 60—65 psi—and if we can just put aside the bias that's fed by our warped sense of male machismo and settle for balls identified as being designed for women—we shall find that they serve much the same purpose and will satisfy the needs of our senior golf swing equally well.

There is another category of golf ball, never mentioned in the statistics of the game or included in the promotional literature of the industry, but one that holds a highly valued and prominent place in the hearts of most amateur players: the found golf ball.

There are two classifications of found golf balls, one group of which is inspired by purely economic considerations. They tend to be good values and are generally available from some golf club pro shops and a few small, privately-owned golf sheds on side streets near the golf course. These balls are usually found by professional scroungers in full diving gear searching bottoms of golf course lakes and are usually sold in bags of 25 or 50 balls per bag…clean and priced according to their condition, but always well below retail.

But that subset of found balls deals only with cash value differentials. The other grouping—with a special emotional appeal totally unrelated to the dollars saved—are those balls found during the game by players on the course. They range from unmarked balls in mint condition to those relics badly yellowed from months in the lake, but whatever their state they are embraced as treasures by their ecstatic finders. Their dollar value may be minimal or even nonexistent, but for the thrill attached to their discovery—in the words of the MasterCard promotion—priceless!

Most of my poker game/golf course friends are reasonably well off, easy-spending and generous, but their course time, when not lining up shots or swinging golf clubs or concocting outlandish bets against their opponent, is spent walking along the shores of the lake or at the edge of the woods looking for lost golf balls. Their joy of success is evident in their broad, victorious grin when reappearing on the fairway with a handful of found balls in conditions varying from fairly good to terrible—even though they are unlikely ever to use many or any of them. There seems to be no sense of logic to the passion, but is probably some sort of inherent, reflexive hoarding instinct tracing back to the golfer's ancient ancestral origins as hunters and gatherers.

For the dedicated and well-equipped scavenger there is another piece of equipment that cannot be overlooked: the Ball Retriever. Few situations are more frustrating than spotting a ball in fairly shallow water, but just beyond your reach. A couple of irons held together in order to grip and recover a submerged ball works pretty well for those balls near the shore, but for a target just beyond that limit you need the benefits of specialization. Ball Retrievers, collapsible poles with some sort of cup or grasping device on the end, come in a range of lengths stretching from 12 feet to 18 feet and sell for prices from about $13 to $35. There is nothing better than a good Ball Retriever for filling empty buckets in the garage with golf balls you are unlikely ever to use. No golf foursome should be without one.

One occasional member of our group, not much of a player but clearly a hunter and gatherer, insists on judging the success of each round by comparing the number of balls found to the number lost and celebrating a positive differential as a victory. Finding five balls, for example, after having lost three, counts as a good day of golf—whatever the number of strokes.

His favorite tale is of the golfer who bragged about having the perfect ball, one with a built-in recovery device. If the ball flies into the lake, for instance, tiny bubbles rise to the surface to make its resting place known to its owner; and if it veers into the woods, it will emit a delicate "beep" to inform the player where to look; and in the falling light of dusk it will glimmer softly to mark its location.

"Why, that's remarkable," marveled his friend. "Where did you get it?"

"I found it."

20

RESOURCES

The best advice for understanding and improving your game is to find a Tom Simon, but failing that (or maybe in addition to that) there are a few books and websites that might help:

BOOKS

Trying to pick and choose from among the thousands of golf books currently extant (there are 3,306 titles on the amazon.com list) is akin to trying to distinguish among the many dimples on a golf ball. Nevertheless, there are a few that I have come across that might prove especially valuable for senior amateur golfers:

Fodor's Golf Digest—identifies 6,000 golf courses around the world, compiled with typical Fodor thoroughness, clarity, and style.

A Good Walk Spoiled by John Feinstein is an inside view of the world of a pro golfer. Although only published in 1995, this book is already a classic. It's a good read and a good book to own, but not necessarily a text book for senior amateur golfers.

Golf Over 40 for Dummies—the age is about right, but the identification is clearly wide of the mark.

Harvey Pennick's Little Red Book, first published in 1992, is an old established classic, venerated by pros and amateurs alike. It is filled with charming and instructive short paragraphs of anecdotes, instructions, and general observations. It's a good book to have in your collection.

It is generally agreed that putting is the most important and most productive golf shot in the game, and Dave Pelz is its premier guru. The two of his best known books, Putting Like a Pro and Putting Bible, along with his Short Game Bible, are worthy of your examination.

Nick Faldo, winner of scores of international golf championships since turning pro in 1977, is recognized as having one of the best, most classic swings in golf, and his book, Faldo—A Swing For Life, illustrates and explains the process exceptionably well.

David Leadbetter is regarded by many pros as one of the game's best instructors, so his books on how to swing, and on finding and fixing faults with your own swing, may be considered a good investment.

Then there are all those books that claim to have it all, like Learn Golf In One Weekend, and The Only Golf Lesson You'll Ever Need, and The Complete Idiot's Guide to Golf, and The Everything Golf Book. After working at the game for better than six decades, and only now reaching my current level of adequacy, I'm inclined to dismiss most of these as a bit overly optimistic, but that is a judgment for you to make.

And it would seem that every pro in the business has written a book, from Julius Boros to Ben Hogan to Jack Nicklaus to Gary Player to Tom Watson to Fred Couple, ad infinitum—and, of course, Tiger Woods. Most of them are good, and some of them are quite good, but those you will have to check out and evaluate for yourselves.

WEBSITES

Generational differences extend well beyond hairstyles or lifestyles or social attitudes or choices of music…or any of the other personal preferences that make up our lives. We live in the Computer Age, which not only changes the way we live and think but has a profound impact on the way in which we gather information—which in turn affects the way we live and think. For the past four or five decades, for example, I hungered for a good set of encyclopedia, but was thwarted by the price until recently when I found and purchased a good used set of the Encyclopedia Britannica. Filled with the joy of my new possession I called my daughter, who was astonished and more than a little critical of my decision, insisting "You can get all the information you could ever want directly from the internet…at a fraction of the time and at no cost."

I'm not about to give up my bias, but she's right, of course. The survival of the printed page is hardly in doubt, but the easy accessibility of information on any topic in whatever form best suits our needs, and in the mind-boggling quantities now freely available on the internet, has radically altered our traditional methods of research.

In this chapter on resources, it was my intention to list the most informative and best constructed golf websites I could find, but my investigation of available sites dissuaded me. Google.com for example, includes more than four million sites advising us on an almost infinite variety of issues related to golf. Yahoo.com offers us a choice of 12 million such websites. Teoma.com quits after only 3.3 million websites. If you're anxious about meeting an early tee-time you can reduce that number of choices by limiting your request to just "Senior Golf Websites" which drops Google's selections down to 215,000 sites, or to Yahoo's 346,000, or to Teoma's mere 86,000. The problem is that many of those websites are website directories, in effect increasing the number of sites available for examination exponentially, producing numbers far beyond my mathematical skills to compute or comprehend.

Coward that I am, I have decided to withhold my advice and leave the search to you, but in order to reduce the quest for the best available sites down to something less thorough but a bit more manageable I provide the following few websites to satisfy your immediate needs. Meanwhile, you had better postpone your tee-time.

One of the more information-packed and valuable sites worth exploration is "www.leaderboard.com." This website provides in-depth information on just about any aspect of the game in which you might be interested, including the Rules, a Glossary, a listing of the Games of Chance, and very much more.

"www.seniorgolfersamerica.com" promotes senior amateur tournaments, along with such special social events as banquets and dances and other assorted get-togethers for the participants. Their individual categories of Senior Golfer include: "Senior" referring to players over 50; "Grand Senior" for players over 70; and "Legendary Senior" for players over 80—which doesn't seem to leave out many players past the age of puberty.

"www.golfonline.com" is the website of "Golf Magazine" and offers much the same information in much the same format as does its printed parent.

"www.thegolfchannel.com" is an extension of television's "Golf Channel" offering a full range of golf information, recommendations and ideas—in content and style rather similar to the golfonline.com site.

"www.golfdiscount.com" is a golf discount website that is about as good as anything my restricted search has been able to find. Their prices seem to be fair (generally well below retail) and they have a full range of all the best brands. It's at least worth a look if you are in the market.

But websites are not just for hustlers (sorry)—for firms that have things to sell. The most prestigious and valuable national golf organizations also have their own websites:

The National Golf Foundation, the industry leader for all relevant information on the business of golf, is extremely informative in all areas of both the amateur and professional aspects of the game. Their web site is "www.ngf.org" and their mailing address is:

The National Golf Foundation

1150 South U.S. Highway One

Jupiter, FL 33477

Phone: (561) 744-6006

fax: (561) 744-6107

The United States Golf Association, has been the national ruling body for golf since 1894, responsible for most of the rules and regulations governing the game both in the United States and worldwide. Their web site is "www.usga.org" or they may be reached at:

The United States Golf Association

Golf House

PO Box 708

Far Hills, NJ 07931-0708

phone: (908) 234-2300

fax: (908) 234-9687

The Professional Golf Association, as the name implies, is the official organization for all aspects of the game as it relates to the professional. Their web site, "www.pga.com," includes just about all the information pertinent to professional golf, from statistics to tournaments to programs…and very much more.

Beyond the listings noted above, each region of the country has it own list of local or statewide golf websites and organizations, divisions that number in the hundreds that can be found through any one of those overburdened search engines listed earlier.

NATIONAL GOLF MAGAZINES:

Golf Digest

PO Box 395

Trumbull, CT 06611-0395

Phone: (203) 373-7000

Fax: (203) 373-7033

Golf Illustrated

5300 CityPlex Tower

2448 East 81st Avenue

Tulsa, OK 74137-5300

Phone: (918) 491-6100

Fax: (918) 491-9424

GOLF Magazine

Two Park Avenue

NY 10016-5695

  Phone: (212) 779-5000

    Fax: (212) 779-5522

Golf Tips

12121 Wilshire Blvd—Suite 1200

Los Angeles, CA 90025-1175

  Phone: (310) 820=1500

    Fax: (310) 826-5008

Golf World US

5520 Park Avenue

Trumbull, CT 06611-3426

  Phone: (203) 373-7000

LINKS—The best of Golf

1040 William Hilton Parkway

Hilton Head Island, SC 29928

  Phone: (803) 842-6200

    Fax:: (803) 842-6233

The Golfer

21 East 40th Street

NY 10016-0501

    Phone: (212) 696-2484

SCORE, Canada's Golf Magazine

287 MacPherson Avenue

Toronto, Ontario M4V 1A4

Canada

    Phone: (416) 928-2909

        Fax: (416) 928-1357

Golf Business Magazine

291 Seven Farms Drive

Charleston, SC 29492

    Phone: 1-800-933-4262 ext. 224

        Fax: 843-856-3288

Travel & Leisure Golf

1942 Broadway—Suite 208

Boulder, CO 80302

    Phone(303)—938-0700

        Fax: (303)—402-6994

21

GLOSSARY OF GOLF TERMS

Ace	hole-in-one
Address	the player's position when preparing to hit the ball
Albatross	score of 2 under par, also known as "double eagle."
Approach shot	a short shot toward the green
Apron	short grass around the green (see Fringe)
Away	player's ball farthest from the hole and his turn to play
Backswing	beginning of the swing—taking the club back (see Takeaway)
Banana ball	a ball hit into the air that curves sharply to the right—like a banana
Baseball grip	using all 10 fingers to hold the club
Best ball	using the best individual score as the team score on a given hole
Birdie	one stroke under par
Bite	backspin on a ball to make it stop quickly when it lands
Blade	a topped shot where the edge of the club hits the ball
Blind hole	a green that cannot be seen because of the dogleg
Bogey	one stroke over par
Bowker	a bad shot headed for trouble that bounces back into play (i.e., "I would have double-bogeyed, but I got a bowker."
Bunker	sand trap
Caddie	The person who carries the player's bag
Cap	top of the club grip and shaft
Carry	the distance the ball travels before hitting down
Casual water	incidental water that is temporary and not part of the course

189

Chili-dip	hitting the ground before hitting the ball (like a Chunk)
Chip shot	A low-trajectory shot used when close to the putting green in order to induce significant roll for maximum control.
Choking down	gripping the club lower than the regular grip
Chunk	(see Chili-dip)
Closed clubface	clubface facing left of the target at the moment of contact with the ball
Closed stance	preparing to hit the ball while standing with the right foot pulled behind behind a line perpendicular to the target. Used for some shots in order to achieve better control.
Collar	the short transitional grass between the fairway and the green (same as the Apron or Fringe)
Divot	a piece dug out of the turf as the result of the swing
Dogleg	a fairly sharp turn of the fairway
Dormie	In match play when a player is ahead by the number of holes remaining
Double bogey	two strokes over par on a hole
Double eagle	three strokes under par on a hole
Downswing	the swing of the club from the top of the backswing back down through the ball
Draw	a controlled shot that curves from right to left
Drop	to place another ball in play when the first one is lost, or to place a ball in a new position in the case of an unplayable lie
Eagle	two stokes under par on one hole
Face	hitting area on the surface of the clubhead
Fade	a controlled shot that curves from left to right
Fat	a mishit where the clubface hits deeply behind the ball
Flange	the thick base of the sand wedge clubhead
Flat swing	a motion in which the club swings more nearly around the body instead of higher above or behind the head
Flop shot	hitting high into the air to reduce the roll upon landing

Follow-through	the completion of the swing after contact
Fringe	the short grass between the fairway and the green (see Apron)
Gimme	a short putt that need not be hit (if all agree)
Grain	the direction grass grows on a green
Gross score	total score taken, excluding handicap strokes
Ground	touching the clubhead to the ground—illegal in a bunker or hazard
Ground under repair	ground marked temporarily unfit for play
Handicap	The number of strokes by which a player can adjust his score to reflect his playing ability. For example, a player with a 15-handicap, shooting a score of 105, would record a net score of 90.
Hanging lie	position of the ball lying below the feet because of the slope of the fairway
Hardpan	densely packed grass or dirt
Hazard	area of the course (sand or water) where you may not ground the club
Heel	the point of the club where the shaft meets the clubhead
Honor	the right to tee off first (usually the winner of the previous hole)
Hood	tilting the clubhead forward (facing toward the ground) while keeping it square to the target
Hook	an uncontrolled flight from right to left
Hosel	the point at which the shaft is inserted into the clubhead
Inside the leather	a ball on the green closer to the hole than the distance from the putter's head to the lower edge of the grip
Lag	purposely hitting a long putt a little short of the hole, seeking a better position for the next shot
Lie	where the ball finally stops
Line	the direction a ball must travel to reach the hole
Lip	the rim of the hole or the edge of the bunker
Lob	a high shot that lands softly

Loft	the angle of the clubface in order to gain more height
Long game	the part of the game played from the tee to (approximately) 125 yards from the green
Match play	a contest between two players on a hole-by-hole basis
Medal play	a competition decided by the best 18-hole total score
Mulligan	a substitute shot for a poorly hit ball
Nassau	a three-part bet—front nine, back nine, and the full eighteen holes
Net score	the final score after deducting handicap strokes
Open clubface	the position when the clubface faces to the right of the target when it meets the ball
Open stance	preparing to hit the ball while standing with the left foot pulled behind behind a line perpendicular to the target
Penalty stroke	an extra stroke assessed for violating a rule or finding relief from a hazard or unplayable lie
Pitch	a short high approach designed to stop with minimum role
Pitch and run	a pitch intended to roll to the hole
Play through	moving ahead of a slower group on the course
Plugged	a ball embedded in the ground
Pot bunker	a small, deep sandtrap
Pro-am	a tournament pairing professional and amateur players
Provisional	hitting a second ball when uncertain of the fate of the first, a stroke that does not count if the first ball is found
Pull	a mishit that flies the ball to the left
Punch	a low, flat shot designed to thwart wind or avoid hindrances
Push	a mishit that flies the ball to the right
Rough	the longer grass along the outsides of the fairway
Rub of the green	golfing term for a run of bad luck
Run up	an approach shot that bounces and rolls toward the hole

Sandbag	a hustle by a good golfer who pretends to play less well than he can
Sand trap	a hazard filled with sand (also called a Bunker)
Sand wedge	an iron with a thick flange, usually used in sand traps
Scramble	a competition in which each member of the team plays the best shot of the team members
Scratch	par golf
Scratch player	a golfer with a handicap of zero
Shaft	the part of the club that connects the clubhead to the grip
Shank	a mishit in which the ball is struck by the hosel and flies right
Short game	the part of the game played within (approximately) 100 yards
Skins game	a competition in which each hole is a separate bet
Skull	to hit near the top of the ball with the leading edge of the club (see Thin)
Sky ball	a ball that flies much higher than anticipated
Slice	an uncontrolled shot that flies to the right of the target
Sole	the bottom of the clubhead
Soleplate	metal plate on the bottom of a wooden club
Stance	the position of the feet at time of address
Stymied	to have an obstruction between your ball and the target
Sweet spot	the part of the clubface that provides the most effective power
Takeaway	the first part of the swing—the start of the backswing
Tee	the stand on which the ball is placed before hitting it
Tee box	the designated place from which to drive the ball
Texas wedge	a name for the putter when used from off the green
Thin	hitting the ball about half way up, making for a low shot (also known as a skulled shot)
Toe	the far end of the clubface
Top	a mishit where the clubface hits the top of the ball

Under club	to use a club inadequate for the distance to be covered
Upright swing	swinging the club high above the shoulder (unlike a Flat swing)
Waggle	the preparatory movement of the club before swinging
Whiff	a complete miss when swinging at the ball
Yips	a psychological impediment to putting

978-0-595-35041-◀
0-595-35041-0

Printed in the United States
30776LVS00003B/1-39